New Chinese
Cooking Class Cookbook

BEEKMAN HOUSE

ISBN 0-517-03077-2
Library of Congress Catalog Card Number: 90-83420

This edition published by Beekman House, Distributed by Outlet Book Company, Inc., a Random House Company, 225 Park Avenue South, New York, NY 10003

Pictured on the front cover: (clockwise from top left): Vegetarian Fried Rice (*page 105*), Shrimp Toast (*page 21*), Barbecued Pork (*page 11*) and Beef with Peppers (*page 38*).

Pictured on the back cover (*from top to bottom*): Wonton Soup (*page 26*), Chinese Chicken Salad (*page 71*), Clams in Black Bean Sauce (*page 91*) and Mongolian Lamb (*page 40*).

CARVAJAL S.A.
Impreso en Colombia
Printed in Colombia

Contents

Introduction

The Chinese are extremely creative in their cooking; it is estimated that there are more than eighty thousand different dishes in Chinese cuisine. But more than that, they show great care in the presentation of their food, believing that food should appeal to more than just the sense of taste. In addition to having good flavor, a dish should be fragrant, colorful and attractive. In a single meal, the various foods should have contrasting textures, and the flavors should maintain a balance between strong and subtle, spicy and bland.

China is a large country, covering over three million square miles in area. The various regions differ widely in climate, terrain and natural resources. These differences determine what kinds of foods are available in a particular region and, as a result, influence the cooking style in that region.

In Chinese cuisine, four regional styles or schools of cooking are generally recognized: northern (including Beijing, Shantung and Anhwei), coastal (Fukien and Shanghai), inland (Szechuan and Hunan) and southern (Canton).

In the relatively cold northern region, wheat—not rice—is the staple food. Noodle dishes,

steamed breads and dumplings are typical fare. Most of the dishes are light and delicate. Garlic and green onions are frequent flavorings, and spices, when used are mild.

The coastal region has produced an abundance of fish and seafood recipes, along with many soups, including, clear, delicious light ones. Dishes from this region are usually well seasoned with soy sauce. In fact, some of the most popular recipes call for meat, poultry or fish to stewed in a liquid that is liberally flavored with soy sauce—a technique often referred to as "red cooking."

In the hot, almost tropical inland region, strongly seasoned spicy foods are preferred. A widely used seasoning is Szechuan pepper, a more potent kind of pepper than the black pepper commonly used in the United States. Deep-fried foods are popular in this region as well.

Many of the Chinese foods familiar to Americans come from the southern region surrounding Canton. Dishes characteristic of the Cantonese style are light, mildly seasoned and less greasy than those of the other regions. Soy sauce, fresh ginger, sherry and chicken broth are the most often used seasonings. People in this

region prefer to taste the natural flavors of the main ingredients of a recipe rather than add extra spices, which is why many Cantonese dishes are prepared using the quick-cooking technique of stir-frying (stir-frying preserves the natural flavors of the foods better than other cooking techniques).

TECHNIQUES FOR CHINESE COOKING

Preparing tasty and attractive Chinese dishes can be a rewarding experience that is easy to accomplish. There are just a few rules to keep in mind for successfully cooking most recipes:

- Preparation and cooking are two separate procedures.
- All ingredients should be prepared *before* any cooking is begun.
- Paying attention to the cooking process is crucial because many of the foods are cooked over intense heat in a matter of minutes.

The Chinese have perfected a variety of cooking techniques, including stir-frying, deep-frying, braising, stewing, steaming, roasting, barbecuing and preserving. Except for stir-frying, all of these techniques are probably familiar to you. To stir-fry correctly, an understanding of its basic principles is necessary.

Stir-frying is a rapid-cooking method invented by the Chinese in ages past when cooking fuel was scarce. It is still the most frequently used of all Chinese cooking techniques. Stir-frying is the brisk cooking of small pieces of ingredients in hot oil over intense heat for a short time, usually just for a few minutes. During cooking, the ingredients must be kept in constant motion by stirring or tossing vigorously. Once cooking is completed, the food should be removed immediately from the heat.

When stir-frying, all of the ingredients must be well organized and prepared *before the cooking is started*. They should be measured or weighed, cleaned, chopped, sliced, combined or the like. The stir-frying is accomplished so quickly that there is usually no time to complete any preparation steps once cooking is begun. Meat, poultry, fish and vegetables should be cut into pieces of approximately the same size for even cooking. Otherwise, one ingredient may be overcooked while others remain undercooked.

The intensity of the heat used for stir-frying is important. In most cases, easily controlled high heat is needed. For this reason, a gas range with its ability for instant heat control is generally more efficient for stir-frying than is an electric range.

The kind of oil used in stir-frying is also crucial. A vegetable oil that can be heated to a high temperature without smoking is essential. Peanut oil, corn oil, cottonseed oil and soybean oil all work well. Other kinds of fats, such as olive oil, sesame oil, butter or lard cannot be used because they have low burning points.

Success in stir-frying depends upon knowing what you are doing and why. Understanding the composition and textures of the ingredients you are using is essential, as is knowing how long each will take to cook—especially in relationship to the others.

Due to the variables that may be involved in stir-frying, such as kinds of foods, type of heat available and the kind of cooking equipment used, cooking times given in this book should be used as guidelines—not as absolutes. Most of the recipes, for example, were tested on a gas range. Cooking times needed when using a wok on an electric range, or when using an electric wok, may vary somewhat.

UTENSILS FOR CHINESE COOKING

A reasonably equipped kitchen usually contains more than enough utensils to adequately handle Chinese cooking. However, one item you may not have, but may wish to consider purchasing, is a wok, especially if you plan to make stir-fried dishes often. Invented many centuries ago, the wok is an all-purpose cooking pan used in virtually every Chinese household for almost every kind of cooking.

Traditionally, a wok was made from thin, tempered iron, and had a rounded bottom for fast, even conduction of heat. However, modern technology has brought some changes to the wok. In addition to iron, woks are now manufactured in aluminum, stainless steel and carbon steel. Woks with flat bottoms are made for use on electric ranges and on smooth-top cooking surfaces. There are electric woks with non-stick finishes and automatic thermostatic controls. On some

woks, the customary thin metal handles positioned on two sides have been replaced with single long wooden handle. This version eliminates the necessity of keeping pot holders handy at all times to pick up or steady the wok. Deciding upon what kind of wok to purchase is a matter of personal preference. All of them are functional.

Woks range in size from 12 to 24 inches in diameter. The 14-inch size is a good choice for use as an all-purpose utensil. That size is adequate to handle most stir-frying and other cooking chores without interfering with the use of other burners on the range top.

Before a new iron or carbon steel wok is used, it should be washed and seasoned. Wash it thoroughly in hot, soapy water (the first time only) and use a scouring pad, if necessary, to remove any protective coating. Rinse the wok with water and dry it completely. Rub 1 tablespoon of vegetable oil completely over the interior of the wok. Place it over low heat until hot throughout, 3 to 5 minutes; remove wok from heat and let cool.

After each use, the wok should be soaked in hot water and cleaned with a bamboo brush or a sponge. Do not clean the wok with soap or soap-treated scouring pads. Rinse the wok with water, dry it and place over low heat until all water evaporates. The rub 1 teaspoon of vegetable oil over the inside of the wok to prevent it from rusting.

Another very useful utensil for Chinese cooking is a cleaver. While not essential, it is handy for slicing, chopping and mincing ingredients, and is especially helpful for chopping whole chickens and ducks into Chinese-style serving pieces (see page 52).

INGREDIENTS IN CHINESE CUISINE

When preparing Chinese foods, you will come across many ingredients that are familiar. You will also encounter some that may be unfamiliar such as hoisin sauce, oyster sauce or Chinese five-spice powder. Some of the items—seasonings in particular—may be available only in Chinese food markets. Before you search for an out-of-the-way specialty store, however, check your local supermarket. Many supermarkets now stock good inventories of Chinese ingredients. In addition to canned, bottled or packages goods, many carry fresh items such as Chinese cabbage (napa or bok choy), bean sprouts, wonton and egg-roll wrappers, bean curd and Chinese-style thin egg noodles. A check of the frozen-food cases will yield additional Chinese items.

As with any other kind of cooking, choose the freshest ingredients you can find, especially when purchasing vegetables, meat, poultry or fish. The Chinese are so conscientious about cooking with the freshest possible foods that they plan their menus around the foods they find in the market—rather than planning the marketing around the menu.

The glossary that follows describes many of the Chinese foods used in the recipes in this book.

GLOSSARY OF CHINESE INGREDIENTS

Bamboo shoots: tender, ivory-colored shoots of tropical bamboo plants, used separately as a vegetable and to add crispness and a slight sweetness to dishes. They are available in cans—whole or sliced—and should be rinsed with water before using.

Barbecue sauce, Chinese: see **Satay sauce**.

Bean curd (also called tofu): pureed soybeans pressed to form a white custard-like cake, used as a vegetable and as an excellent source of protein. Bean curd can be used in all kinds of recipes; although its own flavor is bland, it readily absorbs the flavor of other foods. Bean curd is available fresh or in cans. If fresh, it should be covered with water and stored in the refrigerator.

Bean sprouts: small white shoots of the pea-like mung bean plant, used separately as a vegetable and included in a wide variety of dishes. They are available fresh or in cans. Canned sprouts should be rinsed before use to eliminate any metallic taste. Fresh or opened unused canned sprouts should be covered with water and stored in the refrigerator.

Bean threads (also called Chinese rice vermicelli, transparent or cellophane noodles): dry, hard, white, fine noodles made from powdered mung beans. They have little flavor of their own, but readily absorb the flavors of other foods. Bean threads can be used in numerous steamed, simmered, deep-fried or stir-fried dishes. They are available in packets or small bundles.

Black beans, fermented: strongly flavored, preserved, small black soybeans. They are quite salty and are often used as a seasoning in combination with garlic. Fermented black beans are available in cans, bottles or plastic bags; they should be rinsed or soaked in water before using.

Cabbage, Chinese: there are two types of Chinese cabbages generally available in American markets. One is bok choy, a tender, delicate vegetable with white stalks and green, crinkled leaves. The other is napa cabbage which has elongated tightly furled leaves with wide white ribs and soft pale green tips. Both varieties need very little cooking and are often included in soups and stir-fried dishes.

Cellophane noodles: see **bean threads**

Chili sauce, Chinese: a bright red, extremely spicy sauce made from crushed fresh chili peppers and salt. It is available in cans or bottles and should be used sparingly.

Egg noodles, Chinese-style: thin pasta usually made of flour, egg, water and salt. The noodles can be purchased fresh, frozen or dehydrated. They can be boiled, braised, stir-fried or deep-fried; the time and method of cooking vary with the type of noodle. Check the package for specific instructions.

Egg roll wrappers: commercially prepared dough made of flour and water, rolled very thin, and cut into 7- or 8-inch squares. They are available fresh or frozen.

Five-spice powder, Chinese: cocoa-colored, ready-mixed blend of five ground spices, usually anise seed, fennel, clove, cinnamon and ginger or pepper. It has a slightly sweet, pungent flavor and should be used sparingly.

Ginger (also called ginger root): a knobby, gnarled root, having a brown skin and whitish or light green interior. It has a fresh, pungent flavor and is used as a basic seasoning in many Chinese recipes. Ginger is available fresh or in cans. It will keep for weeks in the refrigerator wrapped in plastic or for months if kept in salted water or dry sherry. There is no adequate substitute for the flavor of fresh ginger—not even ground ginger. Always remove the outer brown skin from fresh ginger before using in any recipe.

Hoisin sauce: a thick, dark brown sauce made of soybeans, flour, sugar, spices, garlic, chili and salt. It has a sweet, spicy flavor and is called for in numerous Chinese recipes.

Lily buds (also called tiger-lily buds or golden needles): long, yellow strips which are the flower buds of the tiger lily. They come dried and must be soaked in warm water before using. Lily buds have a slightly musky flavor and are used in soups, stews and vegetarian dishes. They are available in cellophane packages but can be difficult to find; if you can't get them simply omit them from the recipe.

Lychee (also called lichee or litchi): a small, juicy, oval-shaped fruit with a brownish or bright red skin, white pulp and large pit. They are used in main dishes in combination with other foods or served separately as a dessert or snack. Lychees are available in cans—whole, pitted and packed in syrup.

Mushrooms, dried: dehydrated black or brown mushrooms from the Orient, having caps from 1 to 3 inches in diameter. They have a strong, distinctive flavor and are included in many different kinds of recipes. Chinese dried mushrooms must be soaked in hot water before using; they are usually thinly sliced prior to combining them with other foods. Dried mushrooms are available in cellophane packages.

Oyster sauce: a thick, brown, concentrated sauce made of ground oysters, soy sauce and brine. It imparts very little fish flavor and is used as a seasoning to intensify other flavors. Oyster sauce is included in a variety of recipes, especially in stir-fried Cantonese dishes.

Parsley, Chinese (also called cilantro or fresh coriander): a strongly flavored green herb with flat broad leaves similar in appearance to Italian or flat-leaf parsley. Commonly used fresh as a seasoning or garnish.

Peanut oil: a golden-colored oil pressed from peanuts which has a light and slightly nutty flavor. This oil has a high smoking point which makes it ideal for using in stir-fried recipes. It is available in bottles or cans.

Plum sauce: a thick, piquant chutney-like sauce frequently served with duck or pork dishes. It is available in cans or bottles.

Satay (Saté) sauce (also called Chinese barbecue sauce): a dark brown, hot, spicy sauce composed of soy sauce, ground shrimp, chili peppers, sugar. garlic, oil and spices. It is available in cans or jars.

Sesame oil: an amber-colored oil pressed from toasted sesame seeds. It has a strong, nut-like flavor and is best used sparingly. Sesame oil is generally used as a flavoring, not as a cooking oil because of its low smoking point. It is available in bottles.

Snow peas: (also called pea pods or Chinese peas): flat, green pods that are picked before the peas have matured. They add crispness, color and flavor to foods, require very little cooking and are frequently used in stir-fried dishes. Snow peas are available fresh or frozen.

Soy sauce: a pungent, brown, salty liquid made of fermented soybeans, wheat, yeast, salt and, sometimes, sugar. It is an essential ingredient in Chinese cooking as a seasoning, flavor enhancer for other foods and coloring. There are several types of soy sauces (light, dark, heavy), as well as Japanese-style soy sauce. The Japanese style sauce is somewhere between light and dark varieties. All types of soy sauce are available in bottles.

Szechuan (Sichuan) pepper: a reddish-brown pepper with a strong, pungent aroma and flavor with a time-delayed action—its potent flavor may not be noticed immediately. It comes from the inland Szechuan province and is the main reason the food from that region tends to be hot and spicy. It should be used sparingly. It is usually sold whole or crushed in small packages.

Water chestnut: a walnut-sized bulb from an aquatic plant. The bulb has a tough, brown skin and crisp white interior. Water chestnuts are served separately as a vegetable and are used to add crisp texture and delicate sweet flavor to dishes. They are available whole, peeled fresh, or whole or sliced in cans.

Wonton wrappers: commercially prepared dough that is rolled thinly and cut into 3- to 4-inch squares. They are available fresh or frozen.

Wood ears (also called tree ears or cloud ears): a dried fungus that expands to five or six times its dehydrated size when soaked in warm water. They have a delicate flavor and crunchy texture and are most often used in soups. They are available in cellophane packages.

Appetizers

Stuffed Mushrooms

MUSHROOMS
24 fresh large mushrooms (about 1 pound)
6 ounces boneless lean pork
¼ cup whole water chestnuts (¼ of 8-ounce can)
3 green onions
½ small red or green bell pepper
1 small stalk celery
1 teaspoon cornstarch
1 teaspoon minced fresh ginger
2 teaspoons dry sherry
1 teaspoon soy sauce
½ teaspoon hoisin sauce
1 egg white
Vegetable oil for frying
Batter (recipe follows)
½ cup all-purpose flour

BATTER
½ cup cornstarch
½ cup all-purpose flour
1½ teaspoons baking powder
¾ teaspoon salt
⅓ cup milk
⅓ cup water

1. Clean mushrooms by wiping with a damp paper towel. Remove stems; chop stems finely and transfer to large bowl.

2. Finely chop pork, water chestnuts, onions, red pepper and celery with cleaver or food processor. Add to chopped mushroom stems. Add cornstarch, ginger, sherry, soy sauce, hoisin sauce and egg white; mix well.

3. Spoon pork mixture into mushroom caps, mounding in center. Heat oil in wok or large skillet over high heat to 375°F.

4. For Batter, combine cornstarch, flour, baking powder and salt in medium bowl. Stir in milk and water; blend well.

5. Dip mushrooms in flour, then in batter, coating completely. Cook 6 to 8 mushrooms at a time until golden, about 5 minutes. Drain on paper towels. *Makes 2 dozen*

Green Onion Curls

6 to 8 medium green onions
Cold water
10 to 12 ice cubes

1. Trim bulbs (white part) from onions; reserve for another use. Trim remaining stems (green part) to 4-inch lengths.

2. Using sharp scissors, cut each section of green stems lengthwise into very thin strips down to beginning of stems. Cut 6 to 8 strips in each stem section.

3. Fill large bowl about half full with cold water. Add green onions and ice cubes. Refrigerate until onions curl, about 1 hour. Drain and use for garnish. *Makes 6 to 8 curls*

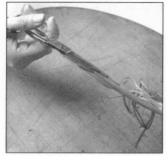

Barbecued Pork ～～～～～～～～～～～～～～～～～

¼ cup soy sauce
2 tablespoons dry red wine
1 tablespoon brown sugar
1 tablespoon honey
2 teaspoons red food coloring (optional)
½ teaspoon ground cinnamon
1 green onion, cut in half
1 clove garlic, crushed
2 whole pork tenderloins (about 12 ounces each), trimmed
Green Onion Curls (recipe follows), for garnish

1. Combine soy sauce, wine, sugar, honey, food coloring, cinnamon, onion and garlic in large bowl. Add pork, turning tenderloins to coat completely. Cover and refrigerate 1 hour or overnight, turning meat occasionally.

2. Drain pork, reserving marinade. Place tenderloins on wire rack over a baking pan. Bake in preheated 350°F oven, turning and basting often with reserved marinade, until cooked through, about 45 minutes.

3. Remove pork from oven; cool. Cut into diagonal slices. Garnish with Green Onion Curls.

Makes about 8 appetizer servings

Dim Sims

8 ounces medium shrimp, shelled, deveined and finely chopped
1 pound boneless lean pork, finely chopped
¼ head small cabbage (about 4 ounces), finely chopped
6 green onions, finely chopped
2 eggs, lightly beaten
3 tablespoons cornstarch
4 teaspoons soy sauce
1 tablespoon sesame oil
2 teaspoons oyster sauce
48 wonton wrappers (about 1 pound)
Vegetable oil for frying

1. Combine shrimp, pork, cabbage and onions in large bowl; mix well. Add eggs, cornstarch, soy sauce, sesame oil and oyster sauce; mix well again.

2. Place rounded teaspoon of mixture onto center of each wonton wrapper.

3. Gently press wrappers around filling, tucking edges together, but leaving tops open. Work with only about 12 wrappers at a time, leaving remaining wrappers covered with plastic wrap or a clean towel.

4. Heat vegetable oil in wok or large skillet over high heat to 375°F. Cook 8 to 10 dim sims at a time until golden, 2 to 3 minutes. Drain on paper towels. *Makes 4 dozen*

Pork and Lettuce Rolls

1 ounce dried mushrooms
1 tablespoon vegetable oil
8 ounces boneless lean pork, finely chopped
½ cup drained sliced bamboo shoots (½ of 8-ounce can), finely chopped
½ cup drained whole water chestnuts (½ of 8-ounce can), finely chopped
6 green onions, finely chopped
1 can (6½ ounces) crab meat, drained and flaked
2 tablespoons dry sherry
1 tablespoon soy sauce
2 teaspoons oyster sauce
2 teaspoons sesame oil
9 iceberg lettuce leaves

1. Place mushrooms in bowl and cover with hot water. Let stand 30 minutes. Drain and squeeze out excess water. Remove and discard stems.

2. Heat vegetable oil in wok or large skillet over high heat. Add pork and stir-fry until golden, 6 to 8 minutes. Add mushrooms, bamboo shoots, water chestnuts, onions and crab meat; stir-fry 1 minute.

3. Combine sherry, soy sauce, oyster sauce and sesame oil. Stir into pork mixture and remove from heat.

4. Place about ⅓ cup pork mixture onto center of each lettuce leaf.

5. Fold ends and sides of lettuce leaves over filling and roll up. Arrange on serving platter. If desired, pork and lettuce leaves may be served separately and rolled at table.

Makes 9 rolls

2

4

5

Pot Stickers

2 cups all-purpose flour
¾ cup plus 2 tablespoons
    boiling water
½ cup very finely chopped napa
    cabbage
8 ounces lean ground pork
2 tablespoons finely chopped
    water chestnuts
1 green onion, finely chopped
1½ teaspoons soy sauce
1½ teaspoons dry sherry
½ teaspoon minced fresh ginger
1½ teaspoons cornstarch
½ teaspoon sesame oil
¼ teaspoon sugar
2 tablespoons vegetable oil,
    divided
⅔ cup chicken broth, divided
    Soy sauce, vinegar and chili
    oil

1. Place flour in large bowl and make a well in center. Pour in boiling water; stir with wooden spoon until dough begins to hold together.

Knead dough until smooth and satiny on lightly floured surface, about 5 minutes. Cover and let rest 30 minutes.

2. For filling, squeeze cabbage to remove as much moisture as possible; place in large bowl. Add pork, water chestnuts, onion, soy sauce, sherry, ginger, cornstarch, sesame oil and sugar; mix well.

3. Divide dough into 2 equal portions; cover 1 portion with plastic wrap or a clean towel while you work with the other portion. Roll out dough to ⅛-inch thickness on lightly floured work surface. Cut out 3-inch circles with round cookie cutter or clean can. Place 1 rounded teaspoon filling in center of each dough circle.

4. To shape each pot sticker, lightly moisten edges of dough circle with water; fold in half. Starting at one end, pinch curled edges together

making 4 pleats along edge. Set dumpling down firmly seam-side up. Cover finished pot stickers while you make remaining dumplings. (Cook dumplings immediately, refrigerate for up to 4 hours or freeze in resealable plastic bag.)

5. To cook pot stickers, heat 1 tablespoon of the vegetable oil in large nonstick skillet over medium heat. Set ½ of pot stickers in pan seam-side up. (If cooking frozen dumplings, do not thaw.) Cook until bottoms are golden brown, 5 to 6 minutes. Pour in ⅓ cup of the chicken broth. Cover tightly, reduce heat and cook until all liquid is absorbed, about 10 minutes (15 minutes if frozen). Repeat with remaining vegetable oil, pot stickers and chicken broth.

6. Place pot stickers browned-side up on serving platter. Serve with soy sauce, vinegar and chili oil for dipping. *Makes 32 pot stickers*

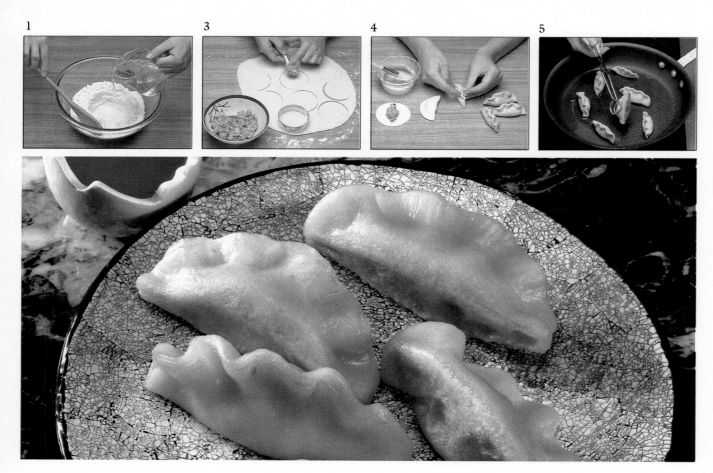

1   3   4   5

Hors d'Oeuvre Rolls

½ cup Chinese-style thin egg
    noodles, broken into 1-inch
    pieces
2 tablespoons butter or
    margarine
4 ounces boneless lean pork,
    finely chopped
6 medium fresh mushrooms,
    finely chopped
6 green onions, finely chopped
8 ounces shelled, deveined
    shrimp, cooked and finely
    chopped
1 hard-cooked egg, finely
    chopped
1½ tablespoons dry sherry
½ teaspoon salt
⅛ teaspoon pepper
2 sheets commercial puff pastry
    dough or 40 wonton
    wrappers
1 egg, beaten
    Vegetable oil for frying
    Sweet and Sour Sauce (see
    page 18), optional

1. Cook noodles according to package directions until tender but still firm, 2 to 3 minutes. Drain and rinse under cold running water and drain again. Chop noodles finely.

2. Heat butter in wok or large skillet over medium-high heat. Add pork and stir-fry until browned, about 5 minutes. Add mushrooms and onions; stir-fry 2 minutes. Remove from heat and add shrimp, hard-cooked egg, cooked noodles, sherry, salt and pepper; mix well.

3. If using puff pastry, roll and trim each sheet into a 15×12-inch rectangle. Cut each rectangle into 20 (3-inch) squares.

4. Place 1 tablespoon pork mixture across center of each pastry square or wonton wrapper. Brush edges lightly with beaten egg. Roll up tightly around filling and pinch edges slightly to seal.

5. Heat oil in wok or large skillet to 375°F. Cook 6 to 8 rolls at a time until golden and crisp, 3 to 5 minutes. Drain on paper towels. Serve with Sweet and Sour Sauce, if desired.

Makes 40 rolls

Spring Rolls

1 pound medium shrimp, shelled, deveined
1 pound boneless lean pork
4 ounces fresh mushrooms
8 green onions
1 red bell pepper
½ head bok choy or napa cabbage (about 8 ounces)
1 can (8 ounces) water chestnuts, drained
3 tablespoons dry sherry
1½ tablespoons soy sauce
2 teaspoons minced fresh ginger
1 teaspoon sugar
½ teaspoon salt
¼ cup water
1½ tablespoons cornstarch
24 spring roll or egg roll wrappers
Vegetable oil for frying

1. Finely chop shrimp, pork, mushrooms, onions, red pepper, cabbage and water chestnuts.

2. Transfer all chopped ingredients to large bowl. Add sherry, soy sauce ginger, sugar and salt; mix well. Blend water and cornstarch in small cup; mix well.

3. Place about ¼ cup pork mixture evenly across one corner of each wrapper. Brush cornstarch mixture evenly over all edges of wrappers. Carefully roll wrappers around filling, folding in corners to seal.

4. Heat oil in wok or large skillet over high heat to 375°F. Cook 3 or 4 rolls at a time until golden, 3 to 5 minutes. Drain on paper towels.

Makes 2 dozen

Fried Wontons

1 ounce dried mushrooms
1 pound boneless lean pork
4 ounces fresh spinach
1½ tablespoons dry sherry
4 teaspoons soy sauce, divided
¼ teaspoon pepper
48 wonton wrappers
 (about 1 pound)
1 can (6 ounces) pineapple juice
½ cup distilled white vinegar
1 tablespoon catsup
½ cup sugar
1½ tablespoons cornstarch
¼ cup water
½ cup Chinese Mixed Pickled
 Vegetables (see page 101)
 Vegetable oil for frying

1. Place mushrooms in bowl and cover with hot water. Let stand 30 minutes. Drain and squeeze out excess water. Cut off and discard stems.

2. Finely chop pork, spinach and mushrooms with cleaver or food processor; transfer to large bowl. Add sherry, 2 teaspoons of the soy sauce and the pepper; mix well.

3. For wontons, work with about 12 wrappers at a time keeping remaining wrappers covered with plastic wrap. Spoon 1 rounded teaspoon pork mixture onto center of each wonton wrapper. Gather edges around filling, pressing firmly at top to seal.

4. Combine pineapple juice, vinegar, catsup, sugar and remaining 2 teaspoons soy sauce in small saucepan. Bring to a boil. Blend cornstarch and water in small cup; stir into pineapple mixture. Reduce heat; cook and stir until thickened, about 3 minutes. Stir in Chinese Mixed Pickled Vegetables; keep warm.

5. Heat oil in wok or large skillet over medium-high heat to 375°F. Cook 8 to 10 wontons at a time until golden and crisp, 2 to 3 minutes. Drain on paper towels. To serve, pour pineapple mixture over wontons. *Makes 4 dozen*

Gow Gees

SWEET AND SOUR SAUCE

1 cup water
½ cup distilled white vinegar
½ cup sugar
¼ cup tomato paste
4 teaspoons cornstarch

GOW GEES

1 ounce dried mushrooms
48 wonton wrappers (about
    1 pound)
2 ounces shelled and deveined
    shrimp
4 ounces boneless lean pork
3 green onions
2 teaspoons soy sauce
½ teaspoon minced fresh ginger
1 clove garlic, crushed
    Vegetable oil for frying

1. For sauce, combine all ingredients in small saucepan. Bring to a boil over medium heat, stirring constantly. Boil and stir 1 minute. Keep warm.

2. For gow gees, place mushrooms in bowl and cover with hot water. Let stand 30 minutes; drain and squeeze out excess water.

3. Cut wonton wrappers into circles using 3-inch cookie cutter or clean can. Cover with plastic wrap.

3

4. Finely chop shrimp, pork, onions and mushrooms with cleaver or food processor; transfer to large bowl. Add soy sauce, ginger and garlic; mix well.

5. Place 1 level teaspoon pork mixture in center of each wonton circle. Brush edges with water. Fold circles in half over filling, pressing edges together to seal.

4

6. Heat oil in wok or large skillet over high heat to 375°F. Cook 8 to 10 gow gees at a time until golden, 2 to 3 minutes. Drain on paper towels. Serve with Sweet and Sour Sauce. *Makes 4 dozen*

6

Ham and Chicken Rolls

2 whole chicken breasts
½ teaspoon salt
¼ teaspoon pepper
¼ teaspoon Chinese five-spice
    powder
⅛ teaspoon garlic powder
4 slices cooked ham (about
    1 ounce each)
1 egg, beaten
2 tablespoons milk
¼ cup all-purpose flour
4 spring roll or egg roll
    wrappers
    Vegetable oil for frying

1. Remove skin from chicken and discard. Cut each breast in half. Remove and discard bones. Using a mallet or rolling pin, pound chicken breasts until very thin.

2. Combine salt, pepper, five-spice powder and garlic powder in small bowl. Sprinkle about ¼ teaspoon spice mixture over each flattened chicken breast.

3. Tightly roll up each ham slice and place on top of chicken; roll chicken around ham, tucking in ends.

4. Combine egg and milk in shallow dish. Coat each chicken piece lightly with flour, then dip into egg-milk mixture. Place each piece diagonally onto a spring roll wrapper. Roll up securely, folding in ends. Brush end corner with egg mixture and pinch to seal.

5. Heat oil in wok or large skillet over high heat to 375°F. Cook 3 or 4 rolls at a time until golden and chicken is cooked through, about 5 minutes. Drain on paper towels. Cool slightly. Cut into 1-inch diagonal slices to serve. *Makes 4 rolls*

3

4

5

Chicken and Banana Squares

2 whole boneless, skinless
   chicken breasts, cooked
2 ripe medium bananas
6 slices white sandwich bread,
   trimmed and quartered
4 eggs
½ cup milk
½ cup all-purpose flour
4 cups soft bread crumbs (10 to
   12 bread slices)
   Vegetable oil for frying

1. Cut chicken breasts into 8 pieces, then cut each of those pieces into thirds, yielding 24 pieces total.

2. Cut each banana lengthwise into quarters. Cut each quarter into thirds, yielding 24 pieces total.

3. Beat eggs and milk in medium bowl until blended. Brush one side of the 24 bread pieces with egg mixture. Place 1 piece of chicken and 1 piece of banana on each egg-glazed bread piece.

4. Place flour in one bowl and soft bread crumbs in another. Coat each chicken-banana square lightly with flour, dip in egg mixture, then coat with bread crumbs. Dip in egg mixture again and coat with crumbs.

5. Heat oil in wok or large skillet over high heat to 375°F. Cook 4 to 6 squares at a time until golden, 2 to 3 minutes. Drain on paper towels.

Makes 2 dozen

Shrimp Toast

12 large shrimp, shelled and deveined, leaving tails intact
1 egg
2½ tablespoons cornstarch
¼ teaspoon salt
  Pinch pepper
3 slices white sandwich bread, crusts removed and quartered
1 hard-cooked egg yolk, cut into ½-inch pieces
1 slice cooked ham, cut into ½-inch pieces
1 green onion, finely chopped
  Vegetable oil for frying

1. Cut down back of shrimp; press gently to flatten. Beat the 1 egg, cornstarch, salt and pepper in large bowl until blended. Add shrimp to egg mixture; toss to coat well.

2. Place 1 shrimp cut-side down on each bread piece. Press shrimp gently into bread. Brush or rub small amount of egg mixture over each shrimp.

3. Place 1 piece each of egg yolk and ham and a scant ¼ teaspoon onion on top of each shrimp.

4. Heat oil in wok or large skillet over medium-high heat to 375°F. Cook 3 or 4 shrimp-bread pieces at a time until golden, 1 to 2 minutes on each side. Drain on paper towels.
Makes 1 dozen

2

3

4

Soups

Mongolian Hot Pot

Mongolian Hot Pot or Chinese Steam-boat — this dish has several names, any of which translate into a meal that's delicious and fun. Traditionally, it's cooked in an Oriental fire pot, which has a chamber under the food basin to hold hot charcoal. This unique pot is not essential to the success of this dish, however. A chafing dish, fondue pot, an electric wok or fry pan are just as functional but less dramatic.

Mongolian Hot Pot is an easy way to entertain because each diner cooks his or her own meal at table. The pot is placed in the center of the table and filled with simmering stock. Each diner chooses his or her own meal from a variety of prepared meat, fish and vegetable offerings then cooks it, piece by piece, in the stock. When all the food has been cooked, the stock (which has become a richly flavored soup) serves as the final course.

Small bowls of assorted Chinese-style accompaniments may be offered, including soy sauce, chili sauce, hoisin sauce, barbecue sauce or lemon sauce. Freshly steamed rice and tea would appropriately round out the meal.

STOCK
10 cups water
2 whole chicken breasts
1 medium yellow onion, sliced
2 stalks celery, cut into ½-inch pieces
1 tablespoon instant chicken bouillon granules
2 tablespoons dry sherry
1 teaspoon sesame oil
1 piece (2×1-inches) fresh ginger, pared and thinly sliced

HOT POT
1 whole beef tenderloin (about 12 ounces)
1 whole pork tenderloin (about 12 ounces)
8 ounces chicken livers, cut into ½-inch slices
2 whole boneless, skinless chicken breasts, cut into 1-inch pieces
1 pound fresh or thawed frozen fish fillets, cut into 1-inch pieces
1 pound medium shrimp, shelled and deveined
24 fresh shucked oysters, optional
½ head small Chinese cabbage, shredded
8 ounces fresh spinach leaves, cut into ½-inch wide strips
8 green onions, cut into 2-inch pieces
1 medium cucumber or zucchini, thinly sliced
1 can (8 ounces) sliced bamboo shoots, drained
8 ounces bean curd, cut into 2×¼-inch slices

1. For stock, combine all stock ingredients in 5-quart stockpot or Dutch oven. Cover and bring to a boil. Reduce heat to low and simmer about 2 hours. Strain stock.

2. For hot pot, wrap beef and pork tenderloins in plastic wrap and freeze 45 to 60 minutes. Cut meat across the grain into ⅛-inch slices. Arrange all meat and fish pieces on serving plates. Cover with plastic wrap and refrigerate until ready to serve.

3. Arrange all vegetables on serving plates; cover with plastic wrap and refrigerate until ready to serve.

4. To prepare fire pot: burn about 24 charcoal briquets in outdoor hibachi or grill until white-hot. Using long-handled tongs, tightly pack coals inside the cooking chamber of the fire pot. Place pot on a thick board to absorb the heat and to protect the tabletop.

5. Heat stock to boiling. Pour into the top of fire pot or other cooking utensil. Uncover trays of prepared meats and vegetables. Provide each diner with small strainers, slotted spoons or chop sticks to hold food. Cook each food by placing in simmering stock until done. Remove and drain slightly; place in individual bowls or plates.

Makes 8 to 10 servings

4

Long Soup

1½ tablespoons vegetable oil
8 ounces boneless lean pork, cut into thin strips
4 to 6 ounces cabbage (¼ of small head), shredded
6 cups chicken broth
2 tablespoons soy sauce
½ teaspoon minced fresh ginger
4 ounces Chinese-style thin egg noodles
8 green onions, diagonally cut into ½-inch slices

1. Heat oil in wok or large skillet over medium-high heat. Add pork and cabbage; stir-fry until pork is cooked through and no longer pink, about 5 minutes.

2. Add chicken broth, soy sauce and ginger to wok. Bring to a boil; reduce heat and simmer 10 minutes.

3. Stir in noodles and onions. Cook just until noodles are tender, 1 to 4 minutes. *Makes about 4 servings*

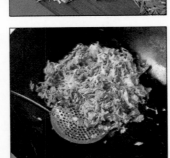

Hot and Sour Soup

3 dried wood ears or 4 dried
    mushrooms
20 dried lily buds, optional
 1 boneless, skinless chicken
    breast half
 1 tablespoon dry sherry
 4 cups chicken broth
½ cup sliced bamboo shoots
    (½ of 8-ounce can),
    drained and cut into
    matchstick pieces
 4 ounces bean curd, drained
    and cut into ½-inch cubes
 3 tablespoons distilled white
    vinegar
 1 tablespoon soy sauce
½ teaspoon ground white
    pepper
 2 tablespoons cornstarch
 3 tablespoons water
 1 egg, lightly beaten
 1 teaspoon sesame oil
 2 green onions, cut into
    1½-inch slivers
 2 tablespoons chopped cilantro
    (Chinese parsley)

1. Place wood ears and lily buds in separate bowls; cover with hot water. Let stand 30 minutes. Drain and squeeze out excess water. Pinch out hard knobs from center of wood ears and discard. Cut wood ears into thin strips. (If using mushrooms, cut off and discard stems; cut caps into thin slices.) Cut off and discard hard tips from lily buds; tie each bud onto itself to make a knot in the middle.

2. Cut chicken crosswise into thin slices; sprinkle with sherry. Let stand 15 minutes.

3. Bring chicken broth to a boil in 3-quart saucepan. Add wood ears, lily buds, chicken and bamboo shoots. Reduce heat and simmer, uncovered, 3 minutes. Add bean curd, vinegar, soy sauce and white pepper; cook 3 minutes more.

4. Blend cornstarch and water in small cup; stir into soup. Cook, stirring, until slightly thickened. Turn off heat. Stirring constantly, slowly pour egg into soup. Stir in sesame oil and onions. Sprinkle with cilantro just before serving.

Makes 4 to 6 servings

1

Wonton Soup

½ cup finely chopped cabbage
4 ounces shelled, deveined shrimp, finely chopped
8 ounces lean ground pork
3 green onions, finely chopped
1 egg, lightly beaten
1½ tablespoons cornstarch
2 teaspoons soy sauce
1 teaspoon oyster sauce
2 teaspoons sesame oil, divided
48 wonton wrappers (about 1 pound)
1 egg white, lightly beaten
¾ pound bok choy or napa cabbage
6 cups chicken broth
1 cup thinly sliced Barbecued Pork (see page 11)
3 green onions, thinly sliced

1. For filling, squeeze cabbage to remove as much moisture as possible. Place cabbage in large bowl. Add shrimp, pork, chopped onions, whole egg, cornstarch, soy sauce, oyster sauce and 1½ teaspoons of the sesame oil; mix well.

2. For wontons, work with about 12 wrappers at a time keeping remaining wrappers covered with plastic wrap. Place 1 wonton wrapper on work surface with one point facing you. Mound 1 teaspoon filling in bottom corner. Fold bottom corner over filling.

3. Moisten side corners with egg white. Bring side corners together, overlapping slightly. Pinch together firmly to seal. Cover finished wontons with plastic wrap while you fill remaining wontons. (Cook immediately, refrigerate up to 8 hours or freeze in resealable plastic bag.)

4. Cut bok choy stems into 1-inch thick slices; cut leaves in half crosswise.

5. Cook wontons in large pot of boiling water until filling is no longer pink, about 4 minutes (6 minutes if frozen). Drain, then place in bowl of cold water to prevent wontons from sticking together.

6. Bring chicken broth to a boil in large saucepan. Add bok choy and remaining ½ teaspoon sesame oil; cook 2 minutes. Drain wontons and add to hot broth. Add slices of Barbecued Pork and sliced onions.

Makes 6 servings

Chicken and Corn Soup

6¾ cups water, divided
2 pounds chicken pieces
1 medium yellow onion, thinly sliced
1 piece fresh ginger (about 1-inch square), pared and thinly sliced
6 whole peppercorns
1½ teaspoons salt, divided
1 or 2 sprigs fresh parsley
8 green onions
1 can (16 ounces) cream-style corn
2 teaspoons instant chicken bouillon granules
1 teaspoon sesame oil
½ teaspoon minced fresh ginger
⅛ teaspoon ground pepper
¼ cup cornstarch
2 egg whites
2 slices cooked ham (about 1 ounce each), cut into 1½-inch strips

1. Combine 6 cups of the water, the chicken pieces, yellow onion, sliced ginger, peppercorns, 1 teaspoon of the salt and the parsley in 5-quart stockpot or Dutch oven. Bring to a boil; reduce heat to low, cover and simmer 1½ hours. Remove any scum or fat from top of stock.

2. Strain stock; return to stockpot. Cut meat from bones and shred with cleaver or knife to yield 1 cup shredded chicken.

3. Finely chop 4 of the green onions. Add chopped onions, corn, bouillon granules, sesame oil, minced ginger, pepper and remaining ½ teaspoon salt to stock. Bring to a boil.

4. Blend cornstarch with ½ cup of the remaining water in small cup. Stir into soup; cook and stir until soup thickens.

5. Beat egg whites and remaining ¼ cup water in small bowl. Stirring constantly, drizzle egg mixture slowly into soup. Stir in ham and shredded chicken.

6. Cut remaining 4 onions into thin slices. Pour soup into bowls; sprinkle with onions.

Makes 6 to 8 servings

Crab Combination Soup

1 ounce dried mushrooms
3 tablespoons cornstarch
6 tablespoons water, divided
1½ tablespoons dry sherry
4 teaspoons soy sauce
1 teaspoon vegetable oil
1 egg, lightly beaten
6 cups chicken broth
6 ounces fresh or thawed
    frozen crab meat, flaked
4 ounces fresh or thawed frozen
    sea scallops, rinsed and
    thinly sliced
½ cup bamboo shoots (½ of
    8-ounce can), drained and
    cut into matchstick pieces
8 green onions, chopped
½ teaspoon minced fresh ginger
2 egg whites

1. Place mushrooms in bowl and cover with hot water. Let stand 30 minutes. Drain and squeeze out excess water. Remove and discard stems; cut caps into thin slices.

2. Combine cornstarch, 4 tablespoons of the water, the sherry and soy sauce in small bowl; mix well and set aside.

3. Heat oil in small skillet over medium-high heat. Add egg and tilt pan to cover bottom. Cook just until egg is set. Loosen edges; turn omelet and cook other side. Remove omelet from pan, roll up and cut into thin strips.

4. Pour broth into 3-quart saucepan. Bring to a boil. Stir in mushrooms, sliced egg, crab meat, scallops, bamboo shoots, onions and ginger. Bring back to a boil.

5. Stir cornstarch mixture; pour into soup. Bring back to a boil. Beat egg whites and remaining 2 tablespoons water in small bowl. Stirring constantly, drizzle egg whites slowly into soup.
Makes 6 servings

Szechuan Soup

1 ounce dried mushrooms
2 quarts chicken stock
½ cup dry white wine
4 teaspoons soy sauce
½ teaspoon Chinese chili sauce
2½ tablespoons cornstarch
5 tablespoons water, divided
6 ounces boneless lean pork,
    cut into matchstick size
    strips
4 ounces cooked ham, cut into
    matchstick size strips
1 small red bell pepper, cut into
    thin strips
½ cup water chestnuts, thinly
    sliced
2 teaspoons distilled white
    vinegar
1 teaspoon sesame oil
1 egg
8 green onions, finely chopped
8 ounces bean curd, cut into
    ½-inch cubes
8 ounces shrimp, shelled and
    deveined

1. Place mushrooms in bowl and cover with hot water. Let stand 30 minutes. Drain and squeeze out excess water. Remove and discard stems. Cut caps into thin slices.

2. Combine chicken stock, wine, soy sauce and chili sauce in 5-quart Dutch oven. Bring to a boil over medium heat. Reduce heat and simmer, uncovered, 5 minutes.

3. Blend cornstarch and 4 tablespoons of the water in small bowl. Slowly stir cornstarch mixture into chicken stock mixture. Cook and stir until soup boils. Add mushrooms, pork, ham, red pepper and water chestnuts. Simmer, uncovered, 5 minutes. Stir vinegar and sesame oil into soup.

4. Beat egg and remaining 1 tablespoon water with fork. Stirring constantly, gradually drizzle egg mixture slowly into soup. Add onions, bean curd, and shrimp. Cook until shrimp turn pink, 1 to 2 minutes.

Makes 6 to 8 servings

Meats

Satay Beef

1 pound beef tenderloin,
    trimmed
5 tablespoons water, divided
1 teaspoon cornstarch
3½ teaspoons soy sauce, divided
1 to 2 teaspoons sesame oil
2 tablespoons vegetable oil
1 medium yellow onion,
    coarsely chopped
1 clove garlic, crushed
1 tablespoon dry sherry
1 tablespoon satay sauce
1 teaspoon curry powder
½ teaspoon sugar

1. Cut beef across the grain into thin slices. Flatten each slice by pressing with fingers.

2. Combine 3 tablespoons of the water, the cornstarch, 1½ teaspoons of the soy sauce and the sesame oil in medium bowl. Add beef; mix to coat well. Let stand 20 minutes.

3. Heat vegetable oil in wok or large skillet over high heat. Add ½ of beef, spreading out slices so they do not overlap. Cook slices on each side just until light brown, 2 to 3 minutes. Remove and set aside. Repeat with remaining meat.

4. Add onion and garlic to wok; stir-fry until onion is soft, about 3 minutes.

5. Combine remaining 2 tablespoons water, 2 teaspoons soy sauce, the sherry, satay sauce, curry powder and sugar in small cup. Add to wok; cook

and stir until liquid boils. Return beef to wok; cook and stir until heated through. *Makes 4 servings*

1

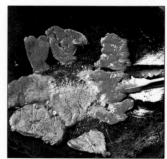

3

5

Beef with Noodles

8 ounces Chinese-style thin egg noodles, cooked and drained
½ cup water
3 teaspoons soy sauce, divided
¼ teaspoon salt
2 teaspoons instant chicken bouillon granules
1 pound beef rump steak, trimmed
6 tablespoons vegetable oil, divided
6 green onions, diagonally sliced
1 piece fresh ginger (about 1 inch square), pared and thinly sliced
2 cloves garlic, crushed

1. Place a clean towel over wire cooling racks. Spread cooked noodles evenly over towel. Let dry about 3 hours.

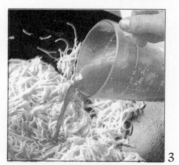

2. Combine water, 2 teaspoons of the soy sauce, the salt and bouillon granules in small bowl. Cut beef across the grain into thin slices about 2-inches long.

3. Heat 4 tablespoons of the oil in wok or large skillet over high heat. Add noodles and stir-fry 3 minutes. Pour water mixture over noodles; toss until noodles are completely coated, about 2 minutes. Transfer noodles to serving plate; keep warm.

4. Heat remaining 2 tablespoons oil in wok over high heat. Add beef, onions, ginger, garlic and remaining 1 teaspoon soy sauce. Stir-fry until beef is cooked through, about 5 minutes. Spoon meat mixture over noodles.

Makes 4 servings

Beef with Black Bean Sauce

1½ pounds beef rump steak, trimmed
2½ tablespoons soy sauce
1½ tablespoons dry sherry
3 teaspoons cornstarch, divided
1 egg white
⅔ cup water, divided
1½ tablespoons fermented, salted black beans
¼ teaspoon sugar
4 tablespoons vegetable oil, divided
4 green onions, cut into 1-inch pieces
1 red bell pepper, thinly sliced
½ cup sliced bamboo shoots (½ of 8-ounce can)
1 teaspoon curry powder

1. Cut beef across the grain into thin slices 2 inches long. Combine soy sauce, sherry, 1 teaspoon of the cornstarch and the egg white in medium bowl; beat lightly. Add beef; stir to coat well. Let stand 30 minutes, stirring occasionally.

2. Combine ⅓ cup of the water and the beans in small bowl. Let stand 15 minutes. Drain beans, reserving 1 teaspoon of the water. Combine beans, reserved water and the sugar on a small plate. Mash well with fork.

3. Heat 2 tablespoons of the oil in wok or large skillet over high heat. Add onions, red pepper, bamboo shoots and curry powder; stir-fry until vegetables are crisp-tender, 2 minutes. Remove and set aside.

4. Combine remaining ⅓ cup water and 2 teaspoons cornstarch in small cup. Heat remaining 2 tablespoons oil in wok over high heat. Add beef and marinade; stir-fry until beef is brown, about 5 minutes. Add vegetables and mashed beans; mix well. Stir in cornstarch mixture. Cook and stir until liquid boils and thickens.

Makes 4 servings

Beef with Cashews

1 pound beef rump steak,
　　trimmed
4 tablespoons vegetable oil,
　　divided
½ cup water
4 teaspoons cornstarch
4 teaspoons soy sauce
1 teaspoon sesame oil
1 teaspoon oyster sauce
1 teaspoon Chinese chili sauce
8 green onions, cut into 1-inch
　　pieces
2 cloves garlic, crushed
1 piece fresh ginger (about
　　1-inch square), pared and
　　finely chopped
⅔ cup unsalted, roasted cashews
　　(about 3 ounces)

1. Cut beef across the grain into thin slices about 2 inches long. Heat 2 tablespoons of the vegetable oil in wok or large skillet over high heat. Stir-fry ½ of beef until brown, 3 to 5 minutes. Remove and set aside. Repeat with remaining beef.

2. Combine water, cornstarch, soy sauce, sesame oil, oyster sauce and chili sauce in small bowl; mix well.

3. Heat remaining 2 tablespoons vegetable oil in wok over high heat. Add onions, garlic, ginger and cashews. Stir-fry 1 minute. Add meat and cornstarch mixture. Cook and stir until liquid boils and thickens. *Makes 4 servings*

1

3

3

Sherried Beef and Spinach

1 pound beef tenderloin,
    trimmed
3 tablespoons dry sherry
1½ tablespoons soy sauce
1 teaspoon sugar
½ teaspoon sesame oil
1 pound fresh spinach, trimmed
3 tablespoons vegetable oil,
    divided
1 piece fresh ginger
    (about 2×1-inch), pared
    and thinly sliced
2 tablespoons water
½ teaspoon cornstarch
1 teaspoon instant chicken
    bouillon granules

1. Cut beef across the grain into thin slices. Cut each slice in half. Flatten slightly by pressing with fingers.

2. Combine sherry, soy sauce, sugar and sesame oil in medium bowl. Add beef; mix to coat well. Cover; refrigerate 2 hours, stirring occasionally.

3. Cut spinach leaves into large pieces. If spinach has thick stems, cut them into ½-inch diagonal slices.

4. Heat 2 tablespoons of the vegetable oil in wok or large skillet over high heat. Add ginger and spinach stems and stir-fry 2 minutes. Remove and set aside.

5. Add remaining 1 tablespoon vegetable oil to wok. Drain meat, reserving marinade. Add ½ of beef to wok spreading out slices so they do not overlap. Cook slices on each side just until light brown, 2 to 3 minutes. Remove and set aside. Repeat with remaining beef.

6. Blend water, cornstarch and bouillon granules into reserved marinade; add to wok. Cook until liquid boils, 1 to 2 minutes. Add spinach leaves, stems and ginger. Stir-fry until spinach is wilted, about 3 minutes. Add beef; stir-fry until heated through, about 1 minute more.

Makes 4 servings

Ginger Beef

2½ tablespoons distilled white
    vinegar
2 teaspoons sugar
½ teaspoon salt
4 ounces fresh ginger, pared
    and thinly sliced
1 pound beef tenderloin,
    trimmed
2 tablespoons dry sherry
2 teaspoons cornstarch
1 teaspoon soy sauce
3 tablespoons vegetable oil,
    divided
1 large green bell pepper, cut
    into 1-inch pieces
6 green onions, cut into 1-inch
    pieces
1 red chili pepper, cut into thin
    slices, for garnish

1. Combine vinegar, sugar and salt in small bowl; stir until sugar dissolves. Add ginger. Let stand 20 to 30 minutes, stirring occasionally.

2. Cut beef across the grain into thin slices about 1½-inches long. Combine sherry, cornstarch and soy sauce in medium bowl. Add beef; stir to coat well. Let stand 20 minutes, stirring occasionally. Drain beef, reserving marinade.

3. Heat 2 tablespoons of the oil in wok or large skillet over high heat. Add ⅓ of beef, spreading slices out so they do not overlap. Cook slices on each side just until light brown, 2 to 3 minutes. Remove and set aside. Repeat twice with remaining beef.

4. Heat remaining 1 tablespoon oil in wok. Add green pepper, onions, ginger mixture and reserved marinade. Stir-fry until vegetables are crisp-tender, 2 to 3 minutes. Return beef to wok. Cook and stir until heated through. Garnish with chili pepper, if desired. *Makes 4 servings*

3

4

Tenderloin Chinese Style

1 pound beef tenderloin
3 tablespoons dry sherry
1½ tablespoons soy sauce
2 teaspoons oyster sauce
1 teaspoon sugar
1 teaspoon cornstarch
½ teaspoon baking soda
¼ teaspoon salt
1 clove garlic, crushed
1½ tablespoons vegetable oil
2 yellow onions, thinly sliced

1. Remove and discard fat from meat. Cut meat across the grain into thin slices.

2. Combine sherry, soy sauce, oyster sauce, sugar, cornstarch, baking soda, salt and garlic in large bowl. Add meat and stir to coat well. Cover and refrigerate at least 3 hours.

3. Heat oil in wok or large skillet over high heat. Add onions and stir-fry until golden, 3 to 5 minutes. Transfer to serving plate; keep warm.

4. Add about ⅓ of the beef to wok, spreading out slices so they do not overlap. Cook slices on each side just until lightly browned, 2 to 3 minutes. Remove from wok and arrange over onions. Repeat with remaining beef. *Makes 4 servings*

Beef with Peppers

1 ounce dried mushrooms
1 pound beef tenderloin,
  trimmed
2½ tablespoons vegetable oil
1 clove garlic, crushed
¼ teaspoon Chinese five-spice
  powder
2 small yellow onions, cut into
  wedges
1 green bell pepper, thinly
  sliced
1 red bell pepper, thinly sliced
¼ cup water
1 tablespoon soy sauce
1 teaspoon cornstarch
1 teaspoon instant beef
  bouillon granules
1 teaspoon sesame oil

1. Place mushrooms in bowl and cover with hot water. Let stand 30 minutes. Drain and squeeze out excess water. Remove and discard stems; slice caps into thin strips.

2. Cut beef into thin slices 1-inch long.

3. Heat vegetable oil in wok or large skillet over high heat. Add garlic and five-spice powder; stir-fry 15 seconds. Add beef and stir-fry until brown, about 5 minutes. Add onions; stir-fry 2 minutes. Add mushrooms and peppers; stir-fry until peppers are crisp-tender, about 2 minutes.

4. Combine remaining ingredients in small bowl. Stir into wok. Cook and stir until liquid boils and thickens.

Makes 4 servings

Curried Beef

1 pound beef tenderloin
3½ tablespoons vegetable oil, divided
2 medium potatoes, cut into ½-inch cubes
2 yellow onions, cut into wedges and separated
4 teaspoons curry powder, divided
⅓ cup water
1 tablespoon cornstarch
2 tablespoons satay sauce
1½ tablespoons soy sauce
1½ tablespoons dry sherry
1 tablespoon Chinese chili sauce
1 teaspoon instant chicken bouillon granules
Steamed Rice (page 104), optional

1. Cut beef across the grain into thin slices. Heat 2½ tablespoons of the oil in wok or large skillet over high heat. Add potatoes and stir-fry until crisp-tender, about 5 minutes. Add onions and 2 teaspoons of the curry powder; stir-fry 2 minutes. Remove and set aside.

2. Heat remaining 1 tablespoon oil in wok over high heat. Add beef slices and stir-fry until light brown, 3 to 4 minutes. Return potato mixture to wok.

3. Combine remaining 2 teaspoons curry powder and remaining ingredients in small cup. Pour into wok; cook and stir until liquid boils. Reduce heat and simmer 3 minutes. Serve with Steamed Rice, if desired. *Makes 4 servings*

Mongolian Lamb

SESAME SAUCE
- 1 tablespoon sesame seeds
- ¼ cup soy sauce
- 1 tablespoon dry sherry
- 1 tablespoon red wine vinegar
- 1½ teaspoons sugar
- 1 clove garlic, minced
- 1 green onion, minced
- ½ teaspoon sesame oil

LAMB
- 1 pound boneless lean lamb (leg or shoulder)
- 2 small leeks, cut into 2-inch slivers
- 4 green onions, cut into 2-inch slivers
- 2 medium carrots, shredded
- 1 medium zucchini, shredded
- 1 red pepper, cut into matchstick pieces
- 1 green bell pepper, cut into matchstick pieces
- ½ small head napa cabbage, thinly sliced
- 1 cup bean sprouts
- 4 tablespoons vegetable oil, divided
- 4 slices pared fresh ginger, divided
- Chili oil, optional

1. For sauce, place sesame seeds in small frying pan. Shake over medium heat until seeds begin to pop and turn golden, about 2 minutes. Let cool. Crush seeds with mortar and pestle (or place on cutting board and crush with a rolling pin; scrape up sesame paste with knife) and transfer to small serving bowl. Add remaining sauce ingredients; mix well.

2. For lamb, slice meat across the grain into strips ¼ inch thick and 2 inches long.

3. Arrange meat and vegetables on large platter. Have Sesame Sauce, vegetable oil, ginger and chili oil near cooking area.

4. At serving time, heat electric griddle or wok to 350°F. Cook one serving at a time. For each serving, heat 1 tablespoon vegetable oil; add 1 slice ginger and cook 30 seconds; discard. Add ½ cup meat strips, stir-fry until lightly browned, about 1 minute. Add 2 cups assorted vegetables; stir-fry 1 minute. Drizzle with 2 tablespoons Sesame Sauce; stir-fry 30 seconds. Season with a few drops chili oil, if desired. Repeat for remaining servings. *Makes 4 servings*

1

2

3

Braised Lion's Head

MEATBALLS
1 pound lean ground pork
4 ounces shrimp, shelled, deveined and finely chopped
¼ cup sliced water chestnuts, finely chopped
1 teaspoon minced fresh ginger
1 green onion, finely chopped
1 tablespoon soy sauce
1 tablespoon dry sherry
½ teaspoon salt
½ teaspoon sugar
1 tablespoon cornstarch
1 egg, lightly beaten
2 tablespoons vegetable oil

SAUCE
1½ cups chicken broth
2 tablespoons soy sauce
½ teaspoon sugar
1 head napa cabbage (1½ to 2 pounds)
2 tablespoons cornstarch
3 tablespoons cold water
1 teaspoon sesame oil

1. For meatballs, combine all meatball ingredients except oil in large bowl; mix well. Divide mixture into 8 portions. Shape each portion into a ball.

2. Heat vegetable oil in wok or large nonstick skillet over medium-high heat. Brown meatballs, shaking or stirring occasionally so meatballs keep their shape, 6 to 8 minutes.

3. Transfer meatballs to 5-quart stockpot; discard drippings. Add chicken broth, soy sauce and sugar. Bring to a boil; reduce heat, cover and simmer 30 minutes.

4. While meatballs are cooking, core cabbage; cut base of leaves into 2-inch squares. Cut leafy tops in half. Place cabbage over meatballs. Cover and simmer 10 minutes more.

5. Using slotted spoon, transfer cabbage and meatballs to serving platter. Blend cornstarch and water in small cup. Stirring constantly, slowly add cornstarch mixture to pan juices; cook until slightly thickened. Stir in sesame oil. To serve, pour sauce over meatballs and cabbage.

Makes 4 to 6 servings

2

4

Steamed Pork Buns

2 tablespoons hoisin sauce
1½ tablespoons oyster sauce
1½ tablespoons soy sauce
½ teaspoon sesame oil
2 tablespoons vegetable oil
2 teaspoons minced fresh ginger
1 clove garlic, crushed
1¼ cups water, divided
1 tablespoon cornstarch
8 ounces Barbecued Pork (page 11), finely chopped
4 green onions, finely chopped
3 cups all-purpose flour
1 tablespoon baking powder
½ teaspoon salt
¼ cup vegetable shortening or lard
1 teaspoon white vinegar

Note: These buns are cooked in bamboo steamers that are available in Chinese and specialty gourmet cookware stores. The round steamers can be purchased in various sizes separately or in sets of two or three tiers. For cooking, the covered steamer(s) is (are) placed over boiling water in a wok or large saucepan.

1. Combine hoisin sauce, oyster sauce, soy sauce and sesame oil in small bowl.

2. Heat vegetable oil in wok or large skillet over high heat. Add ginger and garlic; stir-fry 1 minute. Stir in hoisin sauce mixture; cook and stir 2 minutes. Blend ½ cup of the water and the cornstarch in small cup; stir into wok. Cook and stir until mixture boils. Reduce heat to medium and simmer 2 minutes. Stir in pork and onions. Remove from heat and let cool.

3. Combine flour, baking powder and salt in large bowl. Cut in shortening until mixture resembles bread crumbs. Combine remaining ¾ cup water and the vinegar; stir into flour mixture until dough sticks together. Shape dough into a ball. Knead on lightly floured work surface 6 or 8 times. Cover with plastic wrap and let stand 20 minutes. Uncover and knead 4 or 5 times. Divide dough into 12 equal portions. Shape each portion into a smooth ball.

4. Roll each ball of dough on lightly floured work surface into a 5 to 6-inch diameter circle. Brush around edges lightly with water. Spoon a heaping tablespoon pork mixture onto center of each circle. Carefully pinch edges together to seal dough around filling. Bring the two ends of dough over the seam and pinch together.

5. Cut waxed paper into twelve (5-inch) squares. Brush one side of paper lightly with vegetable oil. Place a bun seam-side down on each square.

6. Place buns with paper in single layer on steamer rack over boiling water. Cover and steam until dough is cooked and filling is hot, about 20 minutes. *Makes 1 dozen*

Sweet and Sour Pork

¼ cup soy sauce
1½ tablespoons dry sherry
2 teaspoons sugar
1 egg yolk
2 pounds boneless lean pork,
    cut into 1-inch pieces
10 tablespoons cornstarch,
    divided
3 cups plus 3 tablespoons
    vegetable oil, divided
1 can (20 ounces) pineapple
    chunks in syrup
¼ cup distilled white vinegar
3 tablespoons tomato sauce
1 cup water
1 large yellow onion, thinly
    sliced
8 green onions, diagonally cut
    into 1-inch pieces
1 red or green bell pepper,
    chopped
4 ounces fresh mushrooms, cut
    into quarters
2 stalks celery, diagonally cut
    into ½-inch slices
1 medium cucumber, seeded
    and cut into ¼-inch wide
    pieces

1. For marinade, combine soy sauce, sherry, sugar and egg yolk in large bowl. Add pork; mix to coat well. Cover and refrigerate 1 hour, stirring occasionally.

2. Drain pork, reserving marinade. Place 8 tablespoons of the cornstarch into large bowl. Add pork pieces; toss to coat well. Heat 3 cups of the oil in wok or large skillet over high heat to 375°F. Add ½ of pork pieces until brown, about 5 minutes. Drain on paper towels. Repeat with remaining pork.

3. Drain pineapple, reserving syrup. Combine the syrup, reserved soy sauce marinade, vinegar and tomato sauce in small bowl. Blend remaining 2 tablespoons cornstarch and the water in another small bowl.

4. Heat remaining 3 tablespoons oil in wok over high heat. Add all vegetables and stir-fry 3 minutes. Add pineapple syrup mixture and cornstarch mixture; cook and stir until sauce boils and thickens. Add pork and pineapple; stir-fry until heated through.   *Makes 4 servings*

2

4

Spiced Pork

3 tablespoons soy sauce,
  divided
2 tablespoons cornstarch
2 tablespoons dry sherry
1 teaspoon minced fresh ginger
½ teaspoon Chinese five-spice
  powder
⅛ teaspoon pepper
2 pounds boneless lean pork,
  cut into large pieces
  Vegetable oil for frying
¼ cup water
1 teaspoon instant chicken
  bouillon granules
  Chinese Mixed Pickled
    Vegetables (see page 101),
    optional

1. Combine 2 tablespoons of the soy sauce, the cornstarch, the sherry, ginger, five-spice powder and pepper in large bowl. Add pork, one piece at a time, turning to coat well. Cover and refrigerate 1 hour, stirring occasionally.

2. Heat oil in wok or large skillet to 375°F. Cook ½ of pork until brown and cooked through, 3 to 5 minutes. Drain on paper towels. Repeat with remaining pork. Cut pork into ¼- to ½-inch wide slices. Transfer to serving dish; keep warm.

3. Combine water, bouillon granules and remaining 1 tablespoon soy sauce in small saucepan. Bring to a boil. Pour mixture over sliced pork. Garnish with Chinese Mixed Pickled Vegetables, if desired.

Makes 4 servings

Mu Shu Pork

8 teaspoons soy sauce, divided
5 teaspoons dry sherry, divided
4 teaspoons cornstarch, divided
8 ounces boneless lean pork,
   cut into matchstick pieces
3 dried mushrooms
2 dried wood ears
7 teaspoons vegetable oil,
   divided
2 eggs, lightly beaten
1 tablespoon water
½ teaspoon sugar
1 teaspoon sesame oil
1 teaspoon minced fresh ginger
½ cup sliced bamboo shoots
   (½ of 8-ounce can), cut
   into matchstick pieces
1 small carrot, shredded
½ cup chicken broth
2 cups bean sprouts (about
   4 ounces)
2 green onions, cut into
   1½-inch slivers
½ cup hoisin sauce
16 Mandarin Pancakes (recipe
   follows)

1. For marinade, combine 2 teaspoons of the soy sauce, 2 teaspoons of the sherry and 1 teaspoon of the cornstarch in large bowl. Add pork and stir to coat. Let stand 30 minutes.

2. Place dried mushrooms and wood ears in small bowl and cover with hot water. Let stand 30 minutes. Drain and squeeze out excess water. Cut off and discard mushroom stems; cut caps into thin slices. Pinch out hard nobs from center of wood ears and discard; cut wood ears into thin strips.

3. Heat ½ teaspoon vegetable oil in small nonstick skillet over medium-high heat. Add ½ of eggs and tilt skillet to cover bottom. Cook just until egg is set. Loosen edges, turn omelet over and cook other side 5 seconds. Remove from skillet and repeat with another ½ teaspoon oil and remaining egg. When omelets are cool, cut in half. Stack halves and cut crosswise into ⅛-inch wide strips.

4. For sauce, combine remaining 6 teaspoons soy sauce, 3 teaspoons sherry and 3 teaspoons cornstarch in small bowl. Add the water, sugar and sesame oil; mix well.

5. Heat remaining 6 teaspoons vegetable oil in wok or large skillet over high heat. Add ginger and stir once. Add pork and stir-fry until meat is no longer pink, about 2 minutes. Add mushrooms, wood ears, bamboo shoots, carrot and chicken broth. Stir and toss 2 minutes. Add bean sprouts and onions; stir-fry 1 minute.

6. Stir cornstarch mixture; pour into wok and cook, stirring constantly, until sauce bubbles and thickens. Stir in omelet strips.

7. To serve, spread about 2 teaspoons hoisin sauce on each pancake. Spoon about 3 tablespoons pork mixture down center. Fold in bottom and roll up.   *Makes 8 servings*

2

3

Mandarin Pancakes

2 cups all-purpose flour
¾ cup boiling water
2 tablespoons sesame oil

1. Place flour in bowl and make a well in center. Pour in boiling water; stir with wooden spoon until dough looks like lumpy meal. Press into a ball. Knead dough until smooth and satiny on lightly floured work surface, about 5 minutes. Cover with clean towel and let rest 30 minutes.

2. Roll dough into 10-inch long log. Cut into 10 equal pieces; keep covered.

3. Cut each piece of dough in half. Roll each half into a ball; flatten slightly. Roll each piece into a 3-inch circle on lightly floured work surface. Brush top of each with a small amount of sesame oil. Stack dough circles together, oil-side in. Roll the pair together into a 6- to 7-inch circle. Repeat for remaining pieces of dough. (Keep uncooked pancakes covered while you roll out remaining dough.)

4. Heat nonstick skillet over medium-low heat. Cook pancakes, 1 pair at a time, turning every 30 seconds, until cakes are flecked with brown and feel dry, 2 to 3 minutes. (Be careful not to overcook; cakes become brittle.)

5. Remove from pan and separate into 2 pancakes while still hot. Stack on plate and keep covered while you cook remaining pancakes. Serve at once, refrigerate or freeze in resealable plastic bag. To reheat, wrap pancakes in clean towel (thaw completely, if using frozen). Steam over simmering water 5 minutes. Fold pancakes into quarters and arrange in serving basket.

Makes 20 pancakes

Two-Onion Pork Shreds

½ teaspoon Szechuan
    peppercorns
4 teaspoons soy sauce, divided
4 teaspoons dry sherry, divided
7½ teaspoons vegetable oil,
    divided
1 teaspoon cornstarch
8 ounces boneless lean pork
2 teaspoons red wine vinegar
½ teaspoon sugar
2 cloves garlic, crushed
½ small yellow onion, cut into
    ¼-inch slices
8 green onions, cut into 2-inch
    pieces
½ teaspoon sesame oil

1. For marinade, place peppercorns in small skillet. Shake over medium-low heat, shaking skillet often, until fragrant, about 2 minutes. Let cool. Crush peppercorns with mortar and pestle (or place between paper towels and crush with a hammer).* Transfer to medium bowl. Add 2 teaspoons of the soy sauce, 2 teaspoons of the sherry, 1½ teaspoons of the vegetable oil and the cornstarch; mix well.

2. Cut pork into ⅛-inch thick slices, then cut into 2×½-inch pieces. Add to marinade and stir to coat well. Let stand 30 minutes.

3. Combine remaining 2 teaspoons soy sauce, 2 teaspoons sherry, the vinegar and sugar in small bowl; mix well.

4. Heat remaining 6 teaspoons vegetable oil in wok or large skillet over high heat. Add garlic and stir once. Add pork and stir-fry until meat is no longer pink, about 2 minutes. Add yellow onion and stir-fry 1 minute; add green onion and stir-fry 30 seconds. Add soy-vinegar mixture and cook 30 seconds. Stir in sesame oil.   *Makes 2 to 3 servings*

*Note: Szechuan peppercorns are deceptively potent. Wear rubber or plastic gloves when crushing them and do not touch your eyes or lips when handling.

Honey-Glazed Spareribs

1 side pork spareribs (about
    2 pounds)
¼ cup plus 1 tablespoon soy
    sauce, divided
3 tablespoons hoisin sauce
3 tablespoons dry sherry,
    divided
1 tablespoon sugar
1 teaspoon minced fresh ginger
2 cloves garlic, minced
¼ teaspoon Chinese five-spice
    powder
2 tablespoons honey
1 tablespoon cider vinegar
    Green Onion Curls (page 10)
    for garnish

1. Have your butcher cut ribs in half lengthwise so that each piece is 2 to 3 inches long. Cut between bones to make 6-inch pieces. Trim excess fat. Place ribs in heavy plastic bag.

2. For marinade, combine ¼ cup of the soy sauce, the hoisin sauce, 2 tablespoons of the sherry, the sugar, ginger, garlic and five-spice powder in small bowl; mix well. Pour marinade over ribs. Seal bag tightly and place in large bowl. Refrigerate 8 hours or overnight, turning bag occasionally.

3. Foil-line a large baking pan. Place rack in pan and place ribs on rack (reserve marinade). Bake in preheated 350°F oven 30 minutes. Turn ribs over, brush with marinade and bake until ribs are tender when pierced with fork, about 40 minutes more.

4. For glaze, combine honey, vinegar, remaining 1 tablespoon soy sauce and 1 tablespoon sherry in small bowl; mix well. Brush ½ of mixture over ribs; place under broiler 4 to 6 inches from heat source and broil until ribs are glazed, 2 to 3 minutes. Turn ribs over, brush with remaining honey mixture and broil until glazed. Cut into serving-size pieces. Garnish with Green Onion Curls, if desired.

Makes about 4 servings

1

3

4

Poultry

Lemon Chicken

CHICKEN
- 4 whole chicken breasts
- ½ cup cornstarch
- ½ teaspoon salt
- ⅛ teaspoon pepper
- ¼ cup water
- 4 egg yolks, lightly beaten
  Vegetable oil for frying
- 4 green onions, sliced

LEMON SAUCE
- 1½ cups water
- ½ cup lemon juice
- 3½ tablespoons brown sugar
- 3 tablespoons cornstarch
- 3 tablespoons honey
- 2 teaspoons instant chicken bouillon granules
- 1 teaspoon minced fresh ginger

1. Remove skin from chicken and discard. Cut chicken breasts in half. Remove and discard bones. Pound with mallet or rolling pin to flatten slightly.

2. Combine cornstarch, salt and pepper in small bowl. Gradually blend in water and egg yolks.

3. Heat oil in wok or large skillet over high heat to 375°F. Dip chicken breasts, one at a time, into cornstarch-egg yolk mixture. Cook chicken breasts, two at a time, until golden, about 5 minutes. Drain on paper towels. Keep warm while cooking remaining chicken.

4. Cut each breast into three or four pieces and arrange on serving plate. Sprinkle with onions.

5. For sauce, combine all sauce ingredients in medium saucepan; mix well. Cook over medium heat, stirring constantly, until sauce boils and thickens, about 5 minutes. Pour over chicken. *Makes 4 to 6 servings*

How to Cut Chicken Chinese-Style

Recipes for Chinese chicken dishes often instruct that chicken be cut into serving-size pieces. These pieces should be smaller than chicken pieces generally are cut. Here are the directions for cutting a whole chicken Chinese-style. A cleaver is the best utensil for chopping a chicken, although a sharp knife or poultry shears may be used.

1. Place chicken breast-side up on a heavy cutting board. Cut in half lengthwise, cutting slightly to one side of the breast bone and the backbone. Cut completely through the chicken to make two pieces. Remove and discard backbone, if desired.

2. Pull each leg up slightly from the breast section. Cut through the ball and socket joint to remove each leg.

3. Cut through the knee joint of each leg to separate into a drumstick and thigh. Pull each wing away from breast and cut through the joint next to the breast.

4. Cut each drumstick, thigh and breast piece crosswise into three pieces, cutting completely through bones. Cut each wing into two pieces.   *Makes 22 small serving-size pieces*

Sesame Chicken Salad

1 tablespoon sesame seeds
3 whole chicken breasts
6 cups water
2 tablespoons soy sauce, divided
½ teaspoon salt
½ teaspoon Chinese five-spice powder
3 stalks celery
1 tablespoon sesame oil
1 tablespoon vegetable oil
¼ teaspoon ground ginger
⅛ teaspoon pepper

1. Sprinkle sesame seeds into small shallow baking pan. Bake in preheated 350°F oven until golden, 5 to 8 minutes.

2. Combine chicken, water, 1 tablespoon of the soy sauce, the salt and five-spice powder in 3- or 4-quart saucepan. Cover and bring to a boil.

Reduce heat and simmer 15 to 20 minutes. Remove from heat. Let stand until chicken is cool enough to handle, about 1 hour.

3. Using slotted spoon, remove chicken and drain (reserve broth). Remove and discard bones. Cut meat into ½-inch wide slices.

4. Cut celery into diagonal slices. Bring reserved cooking broth back to boil. Add celery and cook until crisp-tender, 1 to 2 minutes. Using slotted spoon, remove celery and drain.

5. Combine remaining 1 tablespoon soy sauce, sesame and vegetable oils, ginger and pepper in large bowl. Add chicken and celery; toss to coat well. Transfer to serving bowl. Sprinkle with toasted sesame seeds.

Makes 4 servings

Honey Chili Chicken

1 broiler/fryer chicken
  (3 to 4 pounds)
½ cup all-purpose flour
½ teaspoon salt
  Vegetable oil for frying
⅓ cup water
⅓ cup lemon juice
2 teaspoons cornstarch
4 teaspoons Chinese chili sauce
2 teaspoons soy sauce
1½ teaspoons minced fresh
  ginger
3 tablespoons honey
6 green onions, cut lengthwise
  into thin slices

1. Rinse chicken and cut into small serving-size pieces (see page 52). Combine flour and salt in large bowl. Add chicken pieces and toss to coat well.

2. Heat oil in wok or large skillet over high heat to 375°F. Add chicken, one piece at a time (cook only ⅓ of the pieces at a time), and cook until golden, about 5 minutes. Drain on paper towels. Repeat with remaining chicken.

3. Remove all but 1 tablespoon oil from wok. Combine water, lemon juice, cornstarch, chili sauce and soy sauce in small bowl; mix well.

4. Add ginger to wok; stir-fry 1 minute. Add honey; cook and stir 1 minute. Stir in cornstarch-chili mixture; cook and stir until sauce boils, about 1 minute. Stir in chicken pieces; cook and stir until heated through, about 3 minutes. Stir in onions; cook and stir 1 minute more.

Makes 4 to 6 servings

Chicken with Lychees

3 whole boneless, skinless chicken breasts
¼ cup plus 1 teaspoon cornstarch, divided
3 tablespoons vegetable oil
6 green onions, cut into 1-inch pieces
1 red bell pepper, cut into 1-inch pieces
½ cup tomato sauce
½ cup water, divided
1 teaspoon sugar
1 teaspoon instant chicken bouillon granules
1 can (11 ounces) whole peeled lychees, drained
Vermicelli (page 109), cooked and drained, optional

1. Cut chicken breasts in half; cut each half into 6 pieces. Place ¼ cup of the cornstarch in large bowl. Add chicken pieces and toss to coat well.

2. Heat oil in wok or large skillet over high heat. Add chicken and stir-fry until chicken is light brown, 5 to 8 minutes. Add onions and red pepper; stir-fry 1 minute.

3. Combine tomato sauce, ¼ cup of the water, the sugar and bouillon granules in small bowl; mix well. Pour over chicken-vegetable mixture. Stir in lychees. Reduce heat, cover and cook until chicken is tender, about 5 minutes.

4. Blend remaining ¼ cup water and 1 teaspoon cornstarch in small cup. Stir into chicken mixture. Cook and stir until sauce boils and thickens. Serve with Vermicelli, if desired. *Makes 4 servings*

Chicken with Water Chestnuts

1 ounce dried mushrooms
⅔ cup water
4 teaspoons cornstarch
1 tablespoon instant chicken
    bouillon granules
1 tablespoon dry sherry
1 tablespoon soy sauce
1 tablespoon oyster sauce
1½ cups vegetable oil
2 whole boneless, skinless
    chicken breasts, cut into
    1-inch pieces
3 stalks celery, diagonally cut
    into ½-inch slices
1 red or green bell pepper,
    thinly sliced
1 medium yellow onion, cut
    into wedges and separated
1 can (8 ounces) water
    chestnuts, drained and cut
    into halves
8 ounces bean sprouts
1 piece (about 1 inch square)
    fresh ginger, pared and
    thinly sliced

1. Place mushrooms in medium bowl and cover with hot water. Let stand 30 minutes. Drain and squeeze out excess water. Remove and discard stems; cut caps into halves.

2. Combine water, cornstarch, bouillon granules, sherry, soy sauce and oyster sauce in small bowl; mix well.

3. Heat oil in wok or large skillet over high heat to 375°F. Add chicken pieces, one at a time (cook only ½ of the pieces at a time), and cook until golden, about 5 minutes. Drain on paper towels.

4. Remove all but 2 tablespoons oil from wok. Add mushrooms, celery, red pepper, onion, water chestnuts. bean sprouts, ginger and chicken to wok. Toss to mix well.

5. Stir water mixture and add to wok. Cook and stir until vegetables are crisp-tender, 3 to 5 minutes.

Makes 4 servings

3

4

5

1

2

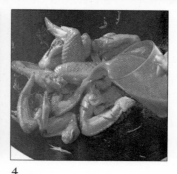

4

Marinated Chicken Wings

3 tablespoons soy sauce
3 tablespoons dry sherry
2 tablespoons brown sugar
1 teaspoon grated fresh ginger
2 cloves garlic, crushed
6 green onions, diagonally cut
    into thin slices
1½ pounds chicken wings, tips
    cut off
2 tablespoons vegetable oil
1 can (8 ounces) sliced bamboo
    shoots, drained
4 teaspoons cornstarch
¾ cup water
1 teaspoon instant chicken
    bouillon granules

1. For marinade, combine soy sauce, sherry, sugar, ginger and garlic in large bowl. Add onions and chicken; toss to coat well. Cover and refrigerate 1 hour, stirring occasionally.

2. Heat oil in wok or large skillet over high heat. Add bamboo shoots and stir-fry 2 minutes. Remove and set aside.

3. Drain chicken and onions, reserving marinade. Add chicken and onions to wok; stir-fry over medium-high heat until chicken is brown, about 5 minutes. Reduce heat to low. Cook until chicken is tender, 15 to 20 minutes.

4. Blend cornstarch and water in small bowl. Stir in bouillon granules and reserved marinade. Add cornstarch mixture to wok. Cook over high heat until liquid boils and thickens. Stir in bamboo shoots. Cook and stir 2 minutes.

Makes 4 servings

Chicken with Mangoes

1 cup all-purpose flour
1¾ cups water, divided
½ teaspoon salt
¼ teaspoon baking powder
3 whole boneless, skinless
    chicken breasts, cut into
    thin strips
    Vegetable oil for frying
1 piece fresh ginger (2×1 inch),
    pared and thinly sliced
3 tablespoons distilled white
    vinegar
3 tablespoons dry sherry
4 teaspoons soy sauce
2 teaspoons sugar
2 teaspoons cornstarch
2 teaspoons instant chicken
    bouillon granules
1 teaspoon sesame oil
8 green onions, cut into ½-inch
    pieces
1 can (15 ounces) mangoes,
    drained and cut into
    ½-inch strips
    Vermicelli (page 109), cooked
    and drained, optional

1. Combine flour, 1 cup of the water, the salt and baking powder in medium bowl. Beat with whisk until blended. Let stand 15 minutes. Add chicken; stir to coat well.

2. Heat vegetable oil in wok or large skillet to 375°F. Add chicken, one strip at a time (cook only about ¼ of the chicken strips at a time), and cook until golden, 3 to 5 minutes. Drain on paper towels. Repeat with remaining chicken.

3. Remove all but 1 tablespoon oil from wok. Reduce heat to medium. Add ginger; stir-fry until light brown, about 2 minutes.

4. Combine remaining ¾ cup water, the vinegar, sherry, soy sauce, sugar, cornstarch, bouillon granules and sesame oil in small bowl. Slowly pour into wok. Cook and stir until sauce boils. Add onions, reduce heat and simmer 3 minutes. Stir chicken and mangoes into wok. Cook and stir 2 minutes. Serve with Vermicelli, if desired. *Makes 4 to 6 servings*

1

4

Asparagus Chicken with Black Bean Sauce

1 tablespoon dry sherry
4 teaspoons soy sauce, divided
5 teaspoons cornstarch, divided
1 teaspoon sesame oil
3 boneless, skinless chicken breast halves, cut into bite-size pieces
1 tablespoon fermented, salted black beans
1 teaspoon minced fresh ginger
1 clove garlic, minced
½ cup chicken broth
1 tablespoon oyster sauce
3 tablespoons vegetable oil, divided
1 pound fresh asparagus spears, trimmed and diagonally cut into 1-inch pieces
1 medium yellow onion, cut into 8 wedges and separated
2 tablespoons water

1. For marinade, combine sherry, 2 teaspoons of the soy sauce, 2 teaspoons of the cornstarch and the sesame oil in large bowl; mix well. Add chicken and stir to coat well. Let stand 30 minutes.

2. Place black beans in sieve and rinse under cold running water. Coarsely chop beans. Combine beans, ginger and garlic; finely chop all three together. Combine chicken broth, remaining 2 teaspoons soy sauce, the oyster sauce and the remaining 3 teaspoons cornstarch in small bowl; mix well and set aside.

3. Heat 2 tablespoons of the vegetable oil in wok or large skillet over high heat. Add chicken and stir-fry until chicken turns opaque, about 3 minutes. Remove and set aside.

4. Heat remaining 1 tablespoon vegetable oil in wok. Add asparagus and onion and stir-fry 30 seconds. Add water; cover and cook, stirring occasionally, until asparagus is crisp-tender, about 2 minutes. Return chicken to wok.

5. Stir chicken broth mixture and add to wok; cook and stir until sauce boils and thickens.

Makes 3 to 4 servings

Spiced Chicken

2 broiler/fryer chickens (3 to
    4 pounds each)
1 cup soy sauce
1 piece (2×1-inches) fresh
    ginger, pared and shredded
2 cloves garlic, crushed
4½ teaspoons Chinese five-spice
    powder, divided
3 tablespoons dry sherry
3 tablespoons honey
1½ tablespoons soy sauce
½ teaspoon sesame oil
    Vegetable oil for frying

FRIED SALT and PEPPER
¼ cup salt
½ teaspoon pepper
1 teaspoon Chinese five-spice
    powder

1. Rinse chickens well and place in large stockpot or Dutch oven. Add enough water to cover chickens. Add the 1 cup soy sauce, ginger, garlic and 4 teaspoons of the five-spice powder. Cover and bring to a boil. Reduce heat and simmer 5 minutes. Turn off heat. Let chickens stand until liquid cools to lukewarm, about 1 hour. Drain chickens.

2. Cut chickens in half lengthwise through center of breast-bone and along back-bone. Drain again and place cut-side down in baking pans.

3. Combine sherry, honey, the 1½ tablespoons soy sauce, the remaining ½ teaspoon five-spice powder and the sesame oil in small bowl. Brush or rub mixture all over chickens.

4. Let chickens stand 2 hours, brushing occasionally with soy-honey mixture.

5. Heat vegetable oil in wok or large skillet over high heat to 375°F. Cook ½ of a chicken at a time until brown, about 2 to 3 minutes on each side. Drain on paper towels. Cut each half chicken into serving-size pieces.

6. For Fried Salt and Pepper, combine salt and pepper in small dry skillet. Cook over medium heat 2 minutes. Stir in 1 teaspoon five-spice powder; cook 1 minute more. Serve as a dip for chicken. *Makes 8 servings*

Beggar's Chicken

1 broiler/fryer chicken (3 to
    4 pounds)
6½ tablespoons soy sauce, divided
2½ tablespoons vegetable oil
2½ tablespoons dry sherry
1 teaspoon sugar
¼ teaspoon Chinese five-spice
    powder
4 green onions, finely chopped
1 piece (about 1-inch square)
    fresh ginger, pared and
    thinly sliced
4 cups all-purpose flour
3 cups salt (about 2 pounds)
1½ to 2 cups water

1. Rinse chicken and pat dry with paper towels. Place chicken on large piece of greased extra-wide heavy-duty aluminum foil. Rub or brush with 2½ tablespoons of the soy sauce. Rub or brush completely with oil. Pull skin at the neck end under chicken and secure with small skewer. Tuck wing tips under chicken.

2. Combine remaining 4 tablespoons soy sauce, the sherry, sugar, five-spice powder, onions and ginger in small bowl. Pour mixture into cavity of chicken, tipping chicken up slightly so mixture does not run out. Secure tail end of chicken with small skewers. Wrap foil around chicken, sealing securely.

3. Combine flour and salt in large bowl. Gradually mix in enough water to make a firm dough. Roll out dough on lightly floured work surface until about ¼-inch thick. Dough should be large enough to completely cover chicken.

4. Place foil-wrapped chicken onto center of dough. Fold dough around chicken, pressing edges together to seal tightly. Place dough-wrapped chicken in well-greased 13×9×2-inch baking dish.

5. Bake chicken in preheated 450°F oven 1 hour. Reduce oven temperature to 300°F. Bake 2½ hours more.

6. Remove chicken from oven. Using mallet or hammer, break pastry. Remove chicken and place on serving plate (discard pastry). Carefully remove foil and skewers.

Makes 4 servings

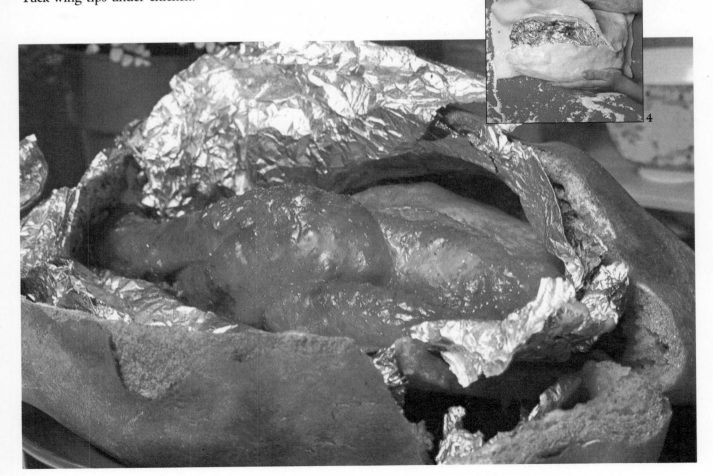

Tea Smoked Chicken

1 teaspoon Szechuan
   peppercorns
2 tablespoons dry sherry
2 tablespoons soy sauce
½ teaspoon granulated sugar
6 thin slices pared fresh ginger
2 green onions, cut into 2-inch
   pieces
1 teaspoon salt
1 broiler/fryer chicken (3 to
   4 pounds)
⅓ cup black tea leaves
3 tablespoons brown sugar
⅓ cup long-grain rice
1 strip dried tangerine peel
   (about 2 inches long) or
   1 teaspoon grated orange
   peel
   Mandarin Pancakes (page 47)
   Prepared plum sauce or
   hoisin sauce
4 green onions, cut into 2-inch
   slivers

1. For marinade, crush peppercorns with mortar and pestle (or place between paper towels and crush with a hammer). Combine crushed peppercorns, sherry, soy sauce, granulated sugar, ginger, onion pieces and salt. Rub chicken inside and out with marinade.* Cover and refrigerate 8 hours or overnight.

2. Place chicken breast-side up on rack in large stockpot. Pour in 1½-inches water. Cover, bring to a boil, and steam until meat near thigh bone is no longer pink, about 45 to 50 minutes. Let stand until cool enough to handle. Lift chicken from rack and drain juices from cavity.

3. Line a large wok and its lid with foil. (Do not use an electric wok with nonstick finish.) For smoking, place tea leaves, brown sugar, rice and tangerine peel in bottom of foil-lined wok; mix well. Set rack on top of mixture in wok. Place chicken breast-side up on rack. Cover wok with foil-lined lid.

4. Cook over high heat 2 minutes. Turn off heat and leave covered 5 minutes. Repeat 2 more times. After final smoking, let stand, covered, to allow smoke to subside, about 30 minutes. Discard smoking mixture.

5. Slice chicken from bones and arrange on serving platter. Serve 1 or 2 chicken slices in Mandarin Pancake; top with plum sauce and slivered onions. *Makes 6 to 8 servings*

*Note: Szechuan peppercorns are deceptively potent. Wear rubber or plastic gloves when rubbing chicken with marinade and do not touch your eyes or lips when handling peppercorns or marinade.

Combination Chop Suey

2 whole chicken breasts, cooked
½ head bok choy or napa
  cabbage (about 8 ounces)
1 cup water
2 teaspoons cornstarch
1 teaspoon chicken bouillon
  granules
4 teaspoons soy sauce
3 tablespoons vegetable oil
8 ounces boneless lean pork,
  finely chopped
4 ounces fresh green beans,
  trimmed and cut into
  ½-inch pieces
3 stalks celery, diagonally cut
  into ½-inch pieces
2 yellow onions, chopped
1 large carrot, finely chopped
8 ounces medium shrimp,
  shelled and deveined
1 can (8 ounces) sliced bamboo
  shoots, drained

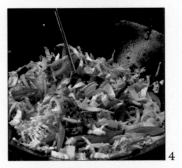

1. Remove skin and bones from cooked chicken. Coarsely chop chicken. Finely chop cabbage with cleaver or large knife.

2. Combine water, cornstarch, boullion and soy sauce in small bowl; set aside.

3. Heat oil in wok or large skillet over high heat. Add pork and stir-fry until brown, about 5 minutes. Remove and set aside.

4. Add cabbage, beans, celery, onions and carrot to wok. Stir-fry until vegetables are crisp-tender, about 3 minutes. Stir soy sauce mixture and pour over vegetables in wok. Cook and stir until liquid boils and thickens, about 3 minutes. Add chicken, shrimp, pork and bamboo shoots. Cook and stir until shrimp turn pink and are cooked through, about 3 minutes more.

Makes 4 to 6 servings

Kung Pao Chicken

5 teaspoons soy sauce, divided
5 teaspoons dry sherry, divided
3½ teaspoons cornstarch, divided
¼ teaspoon salt
3 boneless, skinless chicken breast halves, cut into bite-size pieces
1 tablespoon red wine vinegar
2 tablespoons chicken broth or water
1½ teaspoons sugar
3 tablespoons vegetable oil, divided
⅓ cup salted peanuts
6 to 8 small dried hot chili peppers
1½ teaspoons minced fresh ginger
2 green onions, cut into 1½-inch pieces

1. For marinade, combine 2 teaspoons of the soy sauce, 2 teaspoons of the sherry, 2 teaspoons of the cornstarch and the salt in large bowl; mix well. Add chicken; stir to coat well. Let stand 30 minutes.

2. Combine remaining 3 teaspoons soy sauce, 3 teaspoons sherry, the vinegar, chicken broth, sugar and remaining 1½ teaspoons cornstarch in small bowl; mix well and set aside.

3. Heat 1 tablespoon of the oil in wok or large skillet over medium heat. Add peanuts and cook until golden. Remove and set aside.

4. Heat remaining 2 tablespoons oil in wok over medium heat. Add chili peppers and stir-fry until peppers just begin to char, about 1 minute. Increase heat to high. Add chicken and stir-fry 2 minutes. Add ginger; stir-fry until chicken is cooked through, about 1 minute more. Add onions and peanuts to wok. Stir cornstarch mixture and add to wok; cook and stir until sauce boils and thickens.

Makes 3 servings

Honeyed Chicken and Pineapple

1 broiler/fryer chicken (3 to 4 pounds)
½ cup plus 2 teaspoons cornstarch, divided
Vegetable oil for frying
2 teaspoons minced fresh ginger
1 clove garlic, crushed
1 can (20 ounces) pineapple chunks, drained
1 red or green bell pepper, thinly sliced
1½ cups water
1½ tablespoons honey
1 tablespoon instant chicken bouillon granules
1 teaspoon sesame oil
4 green onions, thinly sliced

1. Rinse chicken and cut into small serving-size pieces (see page 52). Place ½ cup of the cornstarch in large bowl. Add chicken pieces and toss to coat well.

2. Heat oil in wok or large skillet over high heat to 375°F. Add chicken pieces, one at a time (cook only ⅓ of the pieces at a time), and cook until golden and cooked through, about 5 minutes. Drain on paper towels. Repeat with remaining chicken.

3. Remove all but 2 tablespoons oil from wok. Add ginger and garlic and stir-fry 1 minute. Add pineapple and red pepper; stir-fry 2 minutes. Remove and set aside.

4. Combine water and remaining 2 teaspoons cornstarch in small bowl. Blend in honey, bouillon granules and sesame oil. Pour mixture into wok; cook and stir until sauce boils and thickens. Return chicken and pineapple-pepper mixture to wok; cook and stir until heated through. Add green onions; cook and stir 1 minute more. *Makes 4 servings*

Chicken and Chinese Sausages in Clay Pot

6 dried mushrooms
2 tablespoons soy sauce
2 tablespoons dry sherry
1 teaspoon cornstarch
½ teaspoon sugar
¼ teaspoon ground white
　　pepper
2 teaspoons minced fresh
　　ginger, divided
6 boneless, skinless chicken
　　thighs, cut into 1½-inch
　　pieces
1 tablespoon vegetable oil
1 clove garlic, minced
6 ounces Chinese sausages,
　　diagonally cut into ¼-inch-
　　thick slices
½ cup sliced bamboo shoots
　　(½ of 8-ounce can),
　　drained
1½ cups long-grain rice
2¾ cups water
3 green onions, thinly sliced

1. Place mushrooms in medium bowl and cover with hot water. Let stand 30 minutes. Drain and squeeze out excess water. Cut off and discard stems; cut caps into quarters.

2. For marinade, combine soy sauce, sherry, cornstarch, sugar, white pepper and 1 teaspoon of the ginger in large bowl; mix well. Add chicken and stir to coat well. Let stand 30 minutes.

2. Drain chicken, reserving marinade. Heat oil in wok or large skillet over medium high heat. Add garlic and remaining 1 teaspoon ginger; stir-fry 30 seconds. Add chicken; stir-fry until browned, 2 to 3 minutes. Add mushrooms, Chinese sausages, bamboo shoots and reserved marinade. Stir-fry until chicken begins to turn opaque, about 4 minutes. Set aside.

4. Place rice in 3-quart clay pot or saucepan. Add water. Bring to a boil and cook, uncovered, over medium-high heat until crater-like holes form on surface, about 10 minutes.

5. Arrange chicken-sausage mixture on top of rice. Cover and steam over low heat until rice is tender and all liquid is absorbed, about 25 minutes. Sprinkle with onions; serve directly from clay pot.

Makes 4 to 6 servings

1   2   3

Ginger Green Onion Chicken

1 broiler/fryer chicken (3 to
    4 pounds)
1 piece fresh ginger (2×1-inch),
    pared and thinly sliced
1¼ teaspoons salt, divided
½ teaspoon pepper, divided
⅓ cup vegetable oil
8 green onions, finely chopped
3 tablespoons minced fresh
    ginger
2 teaspoons distilled white
    vinegar
1 teaspoon soy sauce
    Steamed Rice (page 104),
    optional

1. Rinse chicken and place in large stockpot or Dutch oven. Add sliced ginger, 1 teaspoon of the salt, ¼ teaspoon of the pepper and enough water to cover chicken. Cover and bring to a boil over high heat. Reduce heat and simmer until tender, about 40 minutes. Let stand until cool.

2. Strain stock and refrigerate or freeze for another use. Refrigerate chicken until cold, then cut into small serving-size pieces (see page 52).

3. Combine remaining ¼ teaspoon salt, ¼ teaspoon pepper, oil, onions, ginger, vinegar and soy sauce in jar with tight-fitting lid. Shake to mix well. Refrigerate 1 to 2 hours.

4. Place chicken in serving bowl. Shake onion-ginger mixture and pour over chicken. Serve with Steamed Rice, if desired.

Makes 4 to 6 servings

Almond Chicken

1½ cups water
4 tablespoons dry sherry, divided
2½ tablespoons cornstarch, divided
4 teaspoons soy sauce
1 teaspoon instant chicken bouillon granules
1 egg white
½ teaspoon salt
4 whole boneless, skinless chicken breasts, cut into 1-inch pieces
Vegetable oil for frying
½ cup blanched whole almonds (about 3 ounces)
1 large carrot, diced
1 teaspoon minced fresh ginger
6 green onions, cut into 1-inch pieces
3 stalks celery, diagonally cut into ½-inch pieces
8 fresh mushrooms, sliced
½ cup sliced bamboo shoots (½ of 8-ounce can), drained

1. Combine water, 2 tablespoons of the sherry, 1½ tablespoons of the cornstarch, the soy sauce and bouillon granules in small saucepan. Cook and stir over medium heat until mixture boils and thickens, about 5 minutes. Keep warm.

2. Combine remaining 2 tablespoons sherry, 1 tablespoon cornstarch, egg white and salt in medium bowl. Add chicken pieces; stir to coat well.

3. Heat oil in wok or large skillet over high heat to 375°F. Add chicken pieces, one at a time (cook only ⅓ of the pieces at a time), and cook until light brown, 3 to 5 minutes. Drain on paper towels. Repeat with remaining chicken.

4. Remove all but 2 tablespoons oil from wok. Add almonds and stir-fry until golden, about 2 minutes; drain.

5. Add carrot and ginger; stir-fry 1 minute. Add all remaining vegetables; stir-fry until crisp-tender, about 3 minutes. Stir in chicken, almonds and sauce; cook and stir until heated through. *Makes 4 to 6 servings*

1

4

5

Hoisin Chicken

1 broiler/fryer chicken (3 to 4 pounds)
½ cup plus 1 tablespoon cornstarch, divided
Vegetable oil for frying
2 teaspoons grated fresh ginger
2 medium yellow onions, chopped
8 ounces fresh broccoli, cut into 1-inch pieces
1 red or green bell pepper, chopped
2 cans (4 ounces each) whole button mushrooms, drained
1 cup water
3 tablespoons dry sherry
3 tablespoons cider vinegar
3 tablespoons hoisin sauce
4 teaspoons soy sauce
2 teaspoons instant chicken bouillon granules

1. Rinse chicken and cut into small serving-size pieces (see page 52). Place ½ cup of the cornstarch in large bowl. Add chicken pieces and toss to coat well.

2. Heat oil in wok or large skillet over high heat to 375°F. Add chicken pieces, one at a time (cook only about ⅓ of the chicken pieces at a time), and cook until golden and cooked through, about 5 minutes. Drain on paper towels. Repeat with remaining chicken.

3. Remove all but 2 tablespoons oil from wok. Add ginger and stir-fry 1 minute. Add onions; stir-fry 1 minute. Add broccoli, red pepper and mushrooms; stir-fry 2 minutes.

4. Combine remaining ingredients and remaining 1 tablespoon corn-starch in small bowl. Add to wok. Cook and stir until sauce boils and turns translucent. Return chicken to wok. Cook and stir until chicken is heated through, about 2 minutes.

Makes 6 servings

Chinese Chicken Salad

2 whole chicken breasts
4 cups water
1 tablespoon dry sherry
2 slices pared fresh ginger
2 whole green onions
¼ cup prepared Chinese plum
    sauce
2 tablespoons distilled white
    vinegar
1 tablespoon vegetable oil
1 tablespoon sesame oil
1½ teaspoons soy sauce
1½ tablespoons sugar
1 teaspoon dry mustard
3 tablespoons slivered almonds
2 tablespoons sesame seeds
4 cups shredded iceberg lettuce
1 small carrot, shredded
1½ cups bean sprouts
    (about 3 ounces)
3 green onions, cut into
    1½-inch slivers
¼ cup cilantro leaves (Chinese
    parsley)
    Bean threads or Vermicelli
    (page 109), cooked and
    drained

1. Combine chicken, water, sherry, ginger and whole green onions in 3-quart saucepan. Bring to a boil; reduce heat, cover and simmer 20 minutes. Remove from heat. Let stand until chicken is cool.

2. Strain stock and refrigerate or freeze for another use. Remove and discard skin and bones from chicken. Pull meat into long shreds.

3. For dressing, combine plum sauce, vinegar, vegetable and sesame oils, soy sauce, sugar and mustard in small bowl; mix well.

4. Place almonds in small dry skillet. Shake over medium heat until golden and fragrant, about 3 minutes. Transfer to large salad bowl. Toast sesame seeds in same skillet until seeds are golden and begin to pop, about 2 minutes. Add sesame seeds to almonds.

5. Add lettuce, carrot, bean sprouts, green onion slivers, cilantro and cooked chicken. Toss to coat evenly. Add bean threads and toss to mix well. *Makes 6 to 8 servings*

Braised Duck

1 ready-to-cook duck (4 to
   5 pounds)
10 tablespoons cornstarch,
   divided
   Vegetable oil for frying
2 cloves garlic, crushed
2 tablespoons dry sherry
2 tablespoons soy sauce,
   divided
1 teaspoon minced fresh ginger
2¾ cups water, divided
2 teaspoons instant chicken
   bouillon granules
1 ounce dried mushrooms
1 can (8 ounces) sliced bamboo
   shoots, drained
1 can (8 ounces) water
   chestnuts, drained
1½ teaspoons sugar
¼ teaspoon pepper
5 green onions, thinly sliced

1. Rinse duck and cut into serving-size pieces (see page 52). Coat pieces with 8 tablespoons of the cornstarch.

2. Heat oil in wok or large skillet over high heat to 375°F. Add garlic and ¼ of the duck pieces, 1 at a time, and cook until brown, about 5 minutes. Drain duck pieces on paper towels. Repeat with remaining duck.

3. Remove oil from wok. Combine sherry, 1 tablespoon of the soy sauce, and the ginger in small bowl; pour over duck. Cook and stir over high heat 2 minutes. Add 2 cups of the water and the bouillon granules. Bring to a boil. Transfer duck and liquid to large saucepan. Cover pan tightly and simmer over low heat until duck is tender, about 1 hour.

4. Meanwhile, place mushrooms in bowl and cover with hot water. Let stand 30 minutes. Drain mushrooms and squeeze out excess water. Remove and discard stems; cut caps into thin slices.

5. Add mushrooms, bamboo shoots and water chestnuts to duck. Cook, stirring often, 5 minutes more.

6. Skim off fat from surface of liquid. Blend remaining ¾ cup water, 2 tablespoons cornstarch, 1 tablespoon soy sauce, the sugar and pepper in small bowl. Stir into duck mixture. Cook and stir over medium heat until liquid boils and thickens, about 4 minutes.   *Makes 6 servings*

Duck with Pineapple

1 ready-to-cook duck
  (4 to 5 pounds)
1¼ cups water, divided
6 tablespoons dry sherry,
  divided
4½ tablespoons distilled white
  vinegar, divided
4½ tablespoons soy sauce, divided
4 tablespoons American-style
  barbecue sauce, divided
¼ teaspoon Chinese five-spice
  powder
1 small ripe pineapple
1 tablespoon cornstarch
2 tablespoons vegetable oil
2 teaspoons minced fresh
  ginger
1 clove garlic, crushed
4 green onions, diagonally cut
  into thin slices
  Green Onion Curls (page
  10), for garnish

1. Rinse duck and place on wire rack in large baking pan. Combine ½ cup of the water, 3 tablespoons *each* of the sherry, vinegar, soy sauce and barbecue sauce, and the ¼ teaspoon five-spice powder in medium bowl; mix well. Pour mixture over duck. Roast duck, uncovered, in preheated 425°F oven, basting and turning often, until light brown, about 20 minutes. Reduce oven temperature to 350°F and roast duck, basting and turning often, 1 hour more. Remove duck from oven; cool completely.

2. Cut duck in half. Remove and discard backbone. Cut duck into small serving-size pieces (see page 52).

3. Twist crown from pineapple. Cut pineapple lengthwise into quarters. Using curved knife, remove fruit from shells. Trim off core and cut fruit into ¼-inch slices.

4. Combine remaining ¾ cup water, 3 tablespoons sherry, 1½ tablespoons *each* vinegar and soy sauce, 1 tablespoon barbecue sauce and the cornstarch in small bowl. Heat oil in wok or large skillet over high heat. Add ginger and garlic and stir-fry 1 minute. Add duck pieces; stir-fry until duck is hot, 3 to 4 minutes. Stir water mixture and pour over duck; cook and stir until sauce boils. Add pineapple slices and onions. Cook and stir until pineapple is hot, about 2 minutes more. Garnish with Green Onion Curls, if desired.

Makes 6 servings

1

2

4

Fish & Seafood

Barbecued Shrimp

1 pound large shrimp, shelled
  and deveined
1 egg white
2 teaspoons cornstarch
1 teaspoon salt
1 cup vegetable oil
1 cup finely chopped yellow
  onions
1 teaspoon curry powder
¼ teaspoon sugar
¼ teaspoon Chinese chili
  powder
¼ cup whipping or heavy cream
2 tablespoons American-style
  barbecue sauce or satay
  sauce
1 small red bell pepper, thinly
  sliced
½ cup brandy, optional

1. Rinse shrimp and pat dry with paper towels. Combine egg white, cornstarch and salt in medium bowl. Add shrimp and stir to coat well. Cover and refrigerate 1 hour.

2. Heat oil in wok or large skillet over medium-high heat to 375°F. Add shrimp, one at a time (cook only about ½ of shrimp at a time), and cook until golden, about 2 minutes. Drain on paper towels.

3. Remove all but 2 tablespoons oil from wok. Add onions, curry powder, sugar and chili powder; stir-fry 2 minutes. Add shrimp; stir-fry 1 minute. Add cream and barbecue sauce; cook and stir 1 minute. Stir in red pepper and remove from heat.

4. Arrange shrimp on serving platter and spoon sauce over shrimp. If desired, heat brandy in small saucepan and pour into small metal bowl on serving platter. Carefully ignite brandy with long wooden match. Hold shrimp over flame for a few seconds. *Makes 2 to 4 servings*

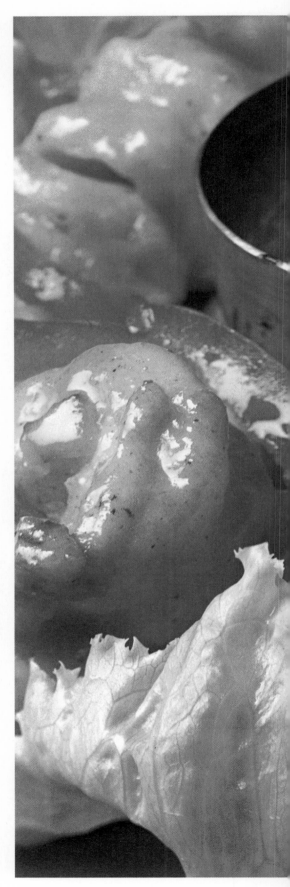

Braised Shrimp with Vegetables

1 tablespoon vegetable oil
1 pound large shrimp, shelled
    and deveined
8 ounces fresh broccoli, cut into
    small pieces
2 cans (4 ounces each) whole
    button mushrooms,
    drained
1 can (8 ounces) bamboo
    shoots, thinly sliced
½ cup chicken broth
1 teaspoon cornstarch
1 teaspoon oyster sauce
¼ teaspoon sugar
½ teaspoon minced fresh ginger
⅛ teaspoon pepper

1. Heat oil in wok or large skillet over high heat. Add shrimp and stir-fry until shrimp turn pink, about 3 minutes.

2. Add broccoli to wok; stir-fry 1 minute. Add mushrooms and bamboo shoots; stir-fry 1 minute more.

3. Combine remaining ingredients in small bowl; mix well. Pour over shrimp-vegetable mixture. Cook and stir until sauce boils and thickens, about 2 minutes more.

Makes 4 servings

Butterfly Shrimp

1½ pounds large shrimp, shelled
    and deveined, leaving tails
    intact
3 egg yolks
1½ teaspoons cornstarch
½ teaspoon salt
⅛ teaspoon pepper
2 slices bacon, cut into 1½×¼-
    inch strips
Vegetable oil for frying

1. Cut deep slit down back of each shrimp. Flatten cut side slightly with fingers.

2. Beat egg yolks, cornstarch, salt and pepper with fork in medium bowl. Dip each shrimp into egg mixture. Place a bacon strip on cut side of each shrimp.

3. Heat oil in wok or large skillet over medium-high heat to 400°F. Cook shrimp, a few at a time, until golden, 2 to 3 minutes. Drain on paper towels.

*Makes 4 to 6 main dish or
8 to 10 appetizer servings*

Shrimp Omelets

3 to 5 tablespoons vegetable oil, divided
8 fresh medium mushrooms, finely chopped
1 cup water
4 teaspoons cornstarch
1 teaspoon sugar
2 teaspoons soy sauce
2 teaspoons instant chicken bouillon granules
8 eggs
½ teaspoon salt
⅛ teaspoon pepper
8 ounces bean sprouts
8 ounces shrimp, shelled, deveined and finely chopped
4 green onions, finely chopped
1 stalk celery, finely chopped
2 green onions, thinly sliced

1. Heat 1 tablespoon of the oil in small skillet. Add mushrooms and cook 1 minute. Remove and set aside.

2. Combine water, cornstarch, sugar, soy sauce and bouillon granules in small saucepan. Cook over medium heat until mixture boils and thickens, about 5 minutes. Keep warm.

3. Combine eggs, salt and pepper in large bowl. Beat until frothy. Add sprouts, shrimp, chopped onions, celery and mushrooms; mix well.

4. For each omelet, heat ½ tablespoon oil in 7-inch omelet pan or skillet. Pour ½ cup egg mixture into pan. Cook until light brown, 2 to 3 minutes on each side. Stack omelets on serving plate. Pour warm soy sauce mixture over omelets. Garnish with sliced onions.

Makes 4 servings

3

3

4

Crab-Stuffed Shrimp

SAUCE

2 tablespoons vegetable oil
1 small yellow onion, finely chopped
1 teaspoon curry powder
1½ tablespoons dry sherry
1 tablespoon satay sauce
1 teaspoon sugar
2 teaspoons soy sauce
¼ cup cream or milk

SHRIMP

2 egg whites
4 teaspoons cornstarch
1 tablespoon dry sherry
1 tablespoon soy sauce
2 cans (6½ ounces each) crab meat, drained and flaked
8 green onions, finely chopped
2 stalks celery, finely chopped
1½ pounds large shrimp, shelled and deveined
½ cup all-purpose flour
3 eggs
3 tablespoons milk
2 to 3 cups soft bread crumbs (8 to 10 bread slices)
Vegetable oil for frying

1. For sauce, heat 2 tablespoons oil in small saucepan over medium heat. Add onion and cook until onion is transparent, about 3 minutes. Add curry powder; cook and stir 1 minute. Add sherry, satay sauce, sugar and soy sauce; cook and stir 2 minutes. Stir in cream; bring to a boil. Boil 2 minutes. Keep warm.

2. For shrimp, blend egg whites, cornstarch, sherry and soy sauce in medium bowl. Add crab meat, onions and celery; mix well.

3. Cut deep slit into but not through back of each shrimp. Flatten shrimp by pounding gently with mallet or rolling pin. Spoon crab mixture onto each shrimp and press with back of spoon or small spatula.

4. Coat each shrimp lightly with flour. Beat eggs and milk with fork in shallow bowl until blended. Place each shrimp stuffed-side up in egg mixture, then spoon mixture over shrimp to cover completely. Coat each shrimp completely with bread crumbs, pressing crumbs lightly onto shrimp. Place shrimp in single layer on cookie sheets or plates. Refrigerate 30 minutes.

5. Heat oil in wok or large skillet over high heat to 375°F. Cook 4 or 5 shrimp at a time until golden, about 3 minutes. Drain on paper towels. Serve with warm sauce.

Makes 4 servings

3

Crab Claws

Sweet and Sour Sauce (page 18)
½ cup Chinese Mixed Pickled Vegetables (page 101)
10 thick crab claws (about 1½ to 2 pounds)
1½ pounds shrimp, shelled and deveined
6 green onions
2 stalks celery
2 teaspoons minced fresh ginger
2 teaspoons soy sauce
2 teaspoons oyster sauce
1 cup cornstarch, divided
½ cup all-purpose flour
½ teaspoon baking powder
½ teaspoon salt
⅔ cup water
Vegetable oil for frying

1. Prepare Sweet and Sour Sauce; stir Chinese Mixed Pickled Vegetables into sauce. Keep warm.

2. Carefully remove the shell from the meat end of each claw using kitchen shears or nut cracker. If necessary, tap claw gently with a mallet or rolling pin to break shell (do not hit heavily or crab meat will be damaged). Leave shell on one part of pincher for holding crab meat.

3. Finely chop shrimp, onions and celery together using cleaver or food processor. Add ginger, soy sauce and oyster sauce; mix well. Divide into 10 equal portions (about ⅓ cup for each portion).

4. Flatten one portion in palm of hand. Place meat end of crab claw on top of flattened shrimp mixture. Carefully press shrimp mixture all around crab meat, leaving shell on pincher uncovered.

5. Place ½ cup of the cornstarch into small bowl. Carefully coat each shrimp-wrapped claw. Combine remaining ½ cup cornstarch, the flour, baking powder and salt in large bowl. Using whisk, blend in water; beat until smooth.

6. Heat oil in wok or large skillet over high heat to 375°F. Carefully dip each crab claw into batter, coating completely. Cook claws, a few at a time, until golden and cooked through, 3 to 5 minutes. Drain on paper towels. Serve with Sweet and Sour Sauce mixture.

Makes 5 servings

Crab in Ginger Sauce

2 ready-to-cook, whole hard-
   shell crabs
¾ cup water, divided
2½ tablespoons dry sherry
1 teaspoon sugar
1 teaspoon instant chicken
   bouillon granules
2 teaspoons soy sauce
2 teaspoons cornstarch
2 tablespoons vegetable oil
½ teaspoon sesame oil
1 piece (about 4×1-inches)
   fresh ginger, pared and cut
   into thin strips
1 red bell pepper, cut into thin
   strips
8 green onions, cut into 1-inch
   pieces

1. Rinse crabs under cold running water. Gently pull away round hard shell on top. With small sharp knife, gently cut away the gray spongy tissue and discard. Rinse again under cold running water.

2. Cut off claws and legs. Pound claws lightly with back of cleaver or hammer to break shells. Chop down center of crab to cut body in half. Cut each half crosswise into 3 pieces.

3. Combine ½ cup of the water, the sherry, sugar, bouillon granules and soy sauce in small bowl; mix well. Blend remaining ¼ cup water and the cornstarch in small cup.

4. Heat vegetable and sesame oils in wok or large skillet over medium heat. Add ginger and stir-fry 1 minute. Add crab pieces; stir-fry 1 minute.

5. Add sherry mixture and red pepper to wok; stir-fry over high heat until liquid boils. Reduce heat, cover and simmer 4 minutes. Stir cornstarch mixture and add to wok. Cook and stir until sauce boils and thickens. Add onions; cook and stir 1 minute more.

Makes 4 to 6 servings

Fish Rolls with Crab Sauce

FISH ROLLS
- 1 pound sole fillets, ¼- to ⅜-inch thick each (about 4 ounces each)
- 1 tablespoon dry sherry
- 2 teaspoons sesame oil
- 1 green onion, minced
- 1 teaspoon minced fresh ginger
- ½ teaspoon salt
  Dash ground white pepper

CRAB SAUCE
- 1½ tablespoons cornstarch
- 2 tablespoons water
- 1 tablespoon vegetable oil
- 1 teaspoon minced fresh ginger
- 2 green onions, thinly sliced
- 1 tablespoon dry sherry
- 6 ounces fresh crab meat, flaked
- 1¼ cups chicken broth
- ¼ cup milk

1. For fish rolls, if fillets are large, cut in half crosswise (each piece should be 5 to 6 inches long). Combine sherry, sesame oil, minced onion, ginger, salt and white pepper in small bowl. Brush each piece of fish with marinade. Let stand 30 minutes.

2. Roll fillets into small bundles. Place on rimmed heatproof dish that will fit inside a steamer. Place dish on rack in steamer. Cover and steam over boiling water until fish turns opaque and flakes easily with fork, 8 to 10 minutes.

3. For crab sauce, blend cornstarch and water in small cup. Heat oil in 2-quart saucepan over medium heat. Add ginger and cook 10 seconds. Add sliced onions, sherry and crab

meat; stir-fry 1 minute. Add chicken broth and milk; bring to a simmer. Stir cornstarch mixture and add to saucepan; cook, stirring, until sauce boils and thickens slightly.

4. Using slotted spoon, transfer fish to serving platter. Pour crab sauce over fish. *Makes 4 to 6 servings*

Seafood Combination

Fried Noodles (see page 111)
4 tablespoons vegetable oil,
    divided
8 green onions, diagonally cut
    into thin slices
3 stalks celery, diagonally cut
    into thin slices
1 can (8 ounces) water
    chestnuts, drained and cut
    into halves
1 can (8 ounces) bamboo
    shoots, thinly sliced
8 ounces fresh or thawed
    frozen sea scallops, cut into
    quarters
8 ounces fresh or thawed
    frozen shrimp, shelled and
    deveined
8 ounces fresh or thawed
    frozen fish fillets, skinned
    and cut into 1½-inch
    square pieces
8 ounces cleaned, ready-to-cook
    squid, optional
½ cup water
1 tablespoon soy sauce
2 teaspoons dry sherry
2 teaspoons cornstarch
1 teaspoon instant chicken
    bouillon granules

1. Prepare Fried Noodles; set aside.

2. Heat 2 tablespoons of the oil in wok or large skillet over high heat. Add onions, celery, water chestnuts and bamboo shoots; stir-fry until crisp-tender, about 2 minutes. Remove and set aside.

3. Heat remaining 2 tablespoons oil in wok over high heat. Add scallops, shrimp, fish pieces and squid; stir-fry until all fish turns opaque and is cooked through, about 3 minutes.

4. Combine water, soy sauce, sherry, cornstarch and bouillon granules in small bowl. Add to wok. Cook and stir until liquid boils. Return vegetables to wok; cook and stir 2 minutes more. Serve with Fried Noodles.

Makes 6 servings

2

4

Scallops with Vegetables

1 ounce dried mushrooms
2 tablespoons vegetable oil
2 yellow onions, cut into
　wedges and separated
3 stalks celery, diagonally cut
　into ½-inch pieces
8 ounces fresh green beans,
　trimmed and diagonally cut
　into 1-inch pieces
2 teaspoons minced fresh
　ginger
1 clove garlic, minced
1 cup water
2½ tablespoons dry sherry
4 teaspoons soy sauce
4 teaspoons cornstarch
2 teaspoons instant chicken
　bouillon granules
1 pound fresh of thawed frozen
　sea scallops, trimmed and
　cut into quarters
6 green onions, diagonally cut
　into thin slices
1 can (15 ounces) baby corn,
　drained

1. Place mushrooms in bowl and cover with hot water. Let stand 30 minutes. Drain and squeeze out excess water. Cut off and discard stems; cut caps into thin slices.

2. Heat oil in wok or large skillet over high heat. Add yellow onions, celery, green beans, ginger and garlic; stir-fry 3 minutes.

3. Combine water, sherry, soy sauce, cornstarch and bouillon granules in medium cup. Add to wok. Cook and stir until sauce boils.

4. Add scallops, mushrooms, green onions and baby corn. Cook and stir until scallops turn opaque, about 4 minutes.　*Makes 4 to 6 servings*

Ginger Chili Fish

SAUCE
- 1 can (8 ounces) tomato sauce
- 2 tablespoons dry sherry
- 1 tablespoon minced fresh ginger
- 1 tablespoon Chinese chili sauce
- 1 tablespoon water
- 1 tablespoon soy sauce
- 2 teaspoons sugar
- 3 cloves garlic, crushed

FISH
- 1 pound fresh or thawed frozen fish fillets
- 1 cup all-purpose flour
- ⅓ cup cornstarch
- ¾ cup water
- 1 egg white
- ½ teaspoon salt
- Vegetable oil for frying

1. For sauce, combine all sauce ingredients in medium saucepan. Bring to a boil; cook and stir 2 minutes. Remove from heat.

2. For fish, remove skin from fillets. (To do this easily, rub some salt on your fingers and grasp skin at tail-end of fish. With a sharp knife held at an angle, separate fish from skin using sawing motion.) Cut fillets into 1-inch pieces.

3. Combine flour, cornstarch, water, egg white and salt. Beat with whisk until smooth.

4. Heat oil in wok or large saucepan over high heat to 375°F. Dip fish pieces, a few at a time, in batter; drain slightly then add to wok and cook until golden, about 5 minutes. Drain on paper towels.

5. Remove oil from wok. Place fish and sauce in wok. Cook over medium heat, tossing lightly, until fish is heated through and coated with sauce, about 2 minutes.

Makes 4 servings

Crispy Fish with Lemon Sauce

LEMON SAUCE
1 cup water
1 piece lemon rind (about 1-inch square)
⅓ cup fresh lemon juice
3 tablespoons brown sugar
1 piece fresh ginger (about 1-inch square) pared and thinly sliced
1 teaspoon instant chicken bouillon granules
1½ tablespoons cornstarch
2 tablespoons water

FISH
¾ cup all-purpose flour, divided
2 whole fish (about 12 ounces each), cleaned and scaled
6 tablespoons water
1½ teaspoons vegetable oil
Vegetable oil for frying
1 egg white
4 green onions, thinly sliced

1. For sauce, combine 1 cup water, lemon rind and juice, sugar, ginger and bouillon in medium saucepan. Bring to a boil. Reduce heat and simmer, uncovered, 5 minutes. Remove from heat, strain sauce and return to saucepan.

2. Blend cornstarch and the 2 tablespoons water in small cup; stir into saucepan. Cook and stir until sauce boils and thickens. Simmer 5 minutes, stirring often. Keep warm.

3. For fish, place ¼ cup of the flour in shallow bowl. Coat fish on both sides with flour. Combine remaining ½ cup flour, the water and 1½ teaspoons vegetable oil in large bowl. Beat with whisk until smooth.

4. Heat vegetable oil in wok or large skillet over high heat to 375°F. Beat egg whites with electric mixer in large bowl until stiff peaks form. Fold whites into batter.

5. Dip one of the whole fish into batter, letting excess drain off. Carefully add fish to wok and cook until golden and cooked through, 8 to 10 minutes. Turn fish over once during cooking. Drain on paper towels. Repeat with second fish.

6. Place fish on serving plate. Stir onions into Lemon Sauce and pour over fish. *Makes 2 servings*

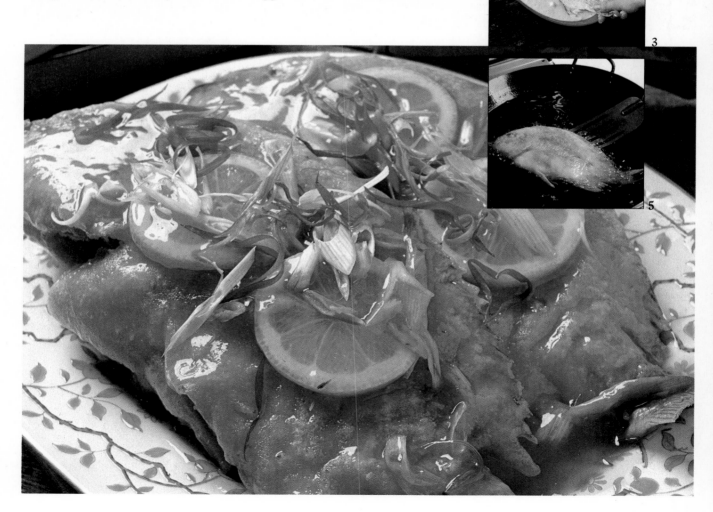

Braised Trout with Sweet and Pungent Sauce

½ cup chicken broth
¼ cup sugar
¼ cup distilled white vinegar
1 tablespoon catsup
1½ teaspoons soy sauce
4 whole cleaned trout
　　(about 8 ounces each)
　　Salt and pepper
¼ cup plus 2 teaspoons
　　cornstarch, divided
3 tablespoons vegetable oil,
　　divided
2 thin slices pared fresh ginger,
　　cut into thin shreds
½ small carrot, shredded
¼ cup sliced bamboo shoots
　　(¼ of 8-ounce can),
　　shredded
¼ cup Chinese mixed pickled
　　vegetables (¼ of 12-ounce
　　jar), sliced
2 green onions, cut into 2-inch
　　slivers
1 tablespoon water

1. For sauce, combine chicken broth, sugar, vinegar, catsup and soy sauce in small bowl; mix well.

2. Sprinkle fish lightly with salt and pepper. Lightly coat using ¼ cup of the cornstarch; shake off excess.

3. Heat 2 tablespoons of the oil in large nonstick skillet over medium-high heat. Add fish and cook until lightly browned, about 2 minutes on each side. Remove and set aside.

4. Discard drippings from skillet and wipe clean with paper towels. Heat remaining 1 tablespoon oil in skillet. Add ginger and stir-fry 10 seconds. Add carrot and bamboo shoots; stir-fry 30 seconds. Return fish to wok. Add pickled vegetables and onions. Pour in chicken broth mixture. Cover and simmer until fish turns opaque and flakes easily with fork, about 3 minutes.

5. While fish is cooking, blend remaining 2 teaspoons cornstarch and the water in small cup. Using slotted spoon, transfer fish to serving platter. Pour cornstarch mixture into wok. Cook and stir until sauce boils and thickens. Spoon sauce over fish.

Makes 4 servings

Chinese Steamed Fish ~~~~~~~~~~~~~~~~~~~~~~~~~~~~~~~~~~

1 fresh whole fish (about
    2 pounds), such as rock
    cod, red snapper or
    kingfish; or 1 pound fish
    fillets or steaks, such as sea
    bass, ling cod, halibut or
    red snapper
1 to 2 teaspoons salt
5 green onions
1 piece fresh ginger (about
    2×1½ inches), pared and
    cut into 1½-inch slivers
2 tablespoons vegetable oil
2 tablespoons soy sauce
    Cilantro sprigs (Chinese
    parsley), for garnish

1. If using whole fish, clean and scale. Make 3 diagonal slashes on each side. Rub fish with 2 teaspoons salt. (If using fillets, rub with 1 teaspoon salt.) Cut 2 of the green onions into 2-inch pieces. Cut the remaining 3 onions into 1½-inch slivers.

2. Place onion pieces in a rimmed heatproof dish that will fit inside a steamer. Place whole fish on top (or place fillets in single layer on top). Place ½ of ginger and ½ of onion slivers on top of fish.

3. Place dish on rack in steamer. Cover and steam over boiling water until fish turns opaque and flakes easily with fork. Steam about 10 minutes per inch of thickness. While fish is cooking, heat oil in small pan until very hot but not smoking.

4. Remove dish from steamer. Pour off about ½ of pan juices. Pour soy sauce over fish. Sprinkle with remaining ginger and onion slivers. Carefully pour hot oil over fish (oil will sizzle.) Garnish with cilantro sprigs. *Makes 4 to 6 servings*

Fragrant Braised Oysters

1 jar (10 or 12 ounces) shucked
  oysters, drained
2 cups plus 1 tablespoon water,
  divided
½ teaspoon salt
¼ cup chicken broth
1 tablespoon dry sherry
1 tablespoon oyster sauce
1 teaspoon cornstarch
¼ teaspoon sugar
2 tablespoons vegetable oil,
  divided
3 slices (about ½-inch each)
  pared fresh ginger, cut into
  thin slivers
½ small yellow onion, cut into
  wedges and separated
3 green onions, cut into 2-inch
  pieces

1. If oysters are large, cut into bite-size pieces. In 2-quart saucepan, bring 2 cups of the water and the salt to a boil. Add oysters. Turn off heat and let stand 30 seconds. Drain, rinse under cold running water and drain again.

2. Combine chicken broth, sherry, oyster sauce, remaining 1 tablespoon water, the cornstarch and sugar in small bowl; mix well.

3. Heat 1 tablespoon of the oil in wok or large skillet over high heat. Add ginger and yellow onion; stir-fry 1 minute. Add green onions; stir-fry 30 seconds. Remove and set aside.

4. Heat remaining 1 tablespoon oil in wok. Add blanched oysters and stir-fry 2 minutes. Return ginger and onions to wok. Stir cornstarch mixture and add to wok. Cook and stir until sauce boils and thickens.

Makes 2 to 3 servings

Clams in Black Bean Sauce

24 small hard-shell clams
1½ tablespoons fermented, salted black beans
2 cloves garlic, minced
1 teaspoon minced fresh ginger
2 tablespoons vegetable oil
2 green onions, thinly sliced
1 cup chicken broth
2 tablespoons dry sherry
1 tablespoon soy sauce
1½ to 2 cups Chinese-style thin egg noodles, cooked and drained
3 tablespoons chopped cilantro (Chinese parsley) or parsley, for garnish

1. Scrub clams under cold running water with stiff brush. (Discard any shells that refuse to close when tapped.)

2. Place black beans in sieve and rinse under cold running water. Coarsely chop beans. Combine beans with garlic and ginger; finely chop all three together.

3. Heat oil in 5-quart pot over medium heat. Add black bean mixture and onions; stir-fry 30 seconds. Add clams and stir to coat.

4. Add chicken broth, sherry and soy sauce to pot. Bring to a boil; reduce heat, cover and simmer until clam shells open, 5 to 8 minutes. (Discard any clams that do not open.)

5. To serve, divide noodles equally among 4 large bowls. Arrange clams on top. Ladle broth over clams. Garnish each serving with chopped cilantro. *Makes 4 servings*

1

2

Vegetables

Chinese Vegetables

1 pound fresh broccoli
¾ cup water
1 tablespoon instant chicken bouillon granules
2 tablespoons vegetable oil
2 medium yellow onions, cut into wedges and separated
1 tablespoon minced fresh ginger
8 ounces fresh spinach, coarsely chopped
8 ounces fresh snow peas or 1 package (6 ounces) thawed frozen snow peas, trimmed and strings removed
4 stalks celery, diagonally cut into ½-inch pieces
8 green onions, diagonally cut into thin slices

1. Cut broccoli tops into florets. Cut stalks into 2×¼-inch thin strips. Combine water and bouillon granules in small cup; mix well.

2. Heat oil in wok or large skillet over high heat. Add broccoli stalks, yellow onions and ginger; stir-fry 1 minute. Add all remaining vegetables; toss lightly.

3. Add water mixture. Toss until vegetables well coated. Bring to a boil, cover and cook until vegetables are crisp-tender, 2 to 3 minutes.
Makes 4 to 6 servings

NOTE: Sliced carrots, zucchini, green beans or green bell peppers may be used in addition to, or in place of, the listed vegetables.

Zucchini Shanghai Style

4 dried mushrooms
½ cup chicken broth
2 tablespoons catsup
2 teaspoons soy sauce
1 teaspoon dry sherry
¼ teaspoon sugar
⅛ teaspoon salt
1 teaspoon red wine vinegar
2 tablespoons vegetable oil, divided
1 teaspoon minced fresh ginger
1 clove garlic, minced
1 green onion, minced
1 large tomato, peeled, seeded and chopped
4 tablespoons water, divided
1 teaspoon cornstarch
1 pound zucchini, diagonally cut into 1-inch pieces
½ small yellow onion, cut into wedges and separated

1. Place mushrooms in bowl and cover with hot water. Let stand 30 minutes. Drain, reserving ¼ cup liquid. Squeeze out excess water. Cut off and discard stems; cut caps into thin slices.

2. Combine the reserved ¼ cup mushroom liquid, the chicken broth, catsup, soy sauce, sherry, sugar, salt and vinegar in small bowl.

3. Heat 1 tablespoon of the oil in 2-quart saucepan over medium-high heat. Add ginger and garlic and stir-fry 10 seconds. Add mushrooms, green onion and tomato. Stir-fry 1 minute. Add chicken broth mixture and bring to a boil; reduce heat and simmer, uncovered, 10 minutes.

4. Blend 1 tablespoon of the water and the cornstarch in small cup. Heat remaining 1 tablespoon oil in wok or large skillet over medium-high heat. Add zucchini and yellow onion and stir-fry 30 seconds. Add remaining 2 tablespoons water, cover and cook, stirring occasionally, until vegetables are crisp-tender, 3 to 4 minutes.

5. Pour tomato sauce into wok. Stir cornstarch mixture and add to wok. Cook and stir until sauce boils and thickens. *Makes 4 to 6 servings*

1

4

Quick Stir-Fried Vegetables

2 cups cauliflower florets
    (about ½ of small head)
3 cups broccoli florets
    (about 1 pound broccoli)
½ small jicama (about 8
    ounces), pared
2 tablespoons vegetable oil
1 teaspoon minced fresh ginger
½ cup chicken broth, divided
¼ teaspoon salt
¼ teaspoon sugar
1 red bell pepper, cut into thin
    strips
1 teaspoon sesame oil

1. Cut a small x in stem end of each cauliflower floret. If florets are large, cut them into 2 or 3 slices. Cut a small x in stem end of broccoli florets. Cut jicama into thick slices, then cut into 2×¼-inch strips. Set all vegetables, oil and seasonings near cooking area.

2. Heat vegetable oil in wok or large skillet over high heat. Add ginger and stir-fry 10 seconds. Add cauliflower and broccoli; stir-fry 30 seconds to coat with oil.

3. Pour about ⅓ cup of the chicken broth around edges of wok. Add salt and sugar. Cover and cook until vegetables are partially tender, 3 to 4 minutes.

4. Add jicama, bell pepper and remaining chicken broth. Cover and cook 1 minute. Uncover and stir-fry until vegetables are crisp-tender and all liquid has evaporated. Stir in sesame oil.   *Makes 4 to 6 servings*

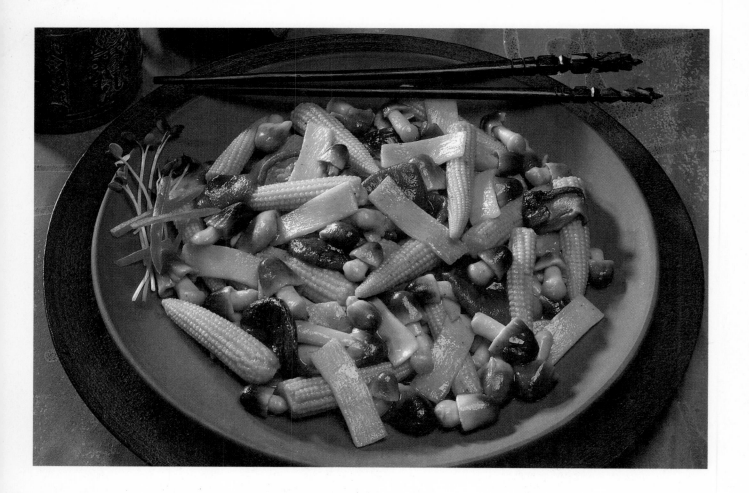

Braised Choice Vegetables

8 dried mushrooms
1 can (15 ounces) peeled straw
   mushrooms
1 cup baby corn (½ of
   15-ounce can)
½ cup sliced bamboo shoots
   (½ of 8-ounce can)
2 tablespoons oyster sauce
2 teaspoons soy sauce
2 tablespoons vegetable oil
1 clove garlic, minced
½ cup chicken broth
2 teaspoons cornstarch
1 tablespoon water

1. Place dried mushrooms in bowl and cover with hot water. Let stand 30 minutes. Drain, reserving ½ cup liquid. Squeeze out excess water. Cut off and discard stems. Leave mushrooms whole, or, if large, cut into halves.

2. Drain straw mushrooms, baby corn and bamboo shoots. If corn is large, diagonally cut each ear into small pieces. Rinse under cold running water and drain. Combine oyster sauce and soy sauce in small cup.

3. Heat oil in wok or large skillet over high heat. Add garlic and stir-fry 10 seconds. Add dried mushrooms; stir-fry 1 minute. Add chicken broth and reserved ½ cup mushroom liquid. Cover and simmer over medium heat until mushrooms are tender and about ½ the liquid has evaporated, about 5 minutes.

4. Add straw mushrooms, corn, bamboo shoots and soy sauce mixture. Simmer 3 minutes. Blend cornstarch and water in small cup. Stir into wok; cook and stir until sauce boils and thickens slightly.

Makes 4 to 6 servings

2

2

Eggplant Szechuan Style

1 pound Oriental eggplants or
    1 domestic eggplant
3 green onions
1 tablespoon minced garlic
2 teaspoons minced fresh
    ginger
2 teaspoons hot bean sauce
½ cup chicken broth
1 tablespoon soy sauce
1 tablespoon red wine vinegar
1½ teaspoons sugar
5 tablespoons vegetable oil,
    divided
1 tablespoon water
1 teaspoon cornstarch
1 teaspoon sesame oil

1. Cut unpeeled eggplant into ½-inch thick slices; cut slices into 2×½-inch strips.

2. Cut 1 of the green onions into thin slices; reserve for garnish. Cut remaining 2 green onions into thin slices. Combine onions, garlic, ginger and hot bean sauce in medium bowl. Combine chicken broth, soy sauce, vinegar and sugar in small bowl.

3. Heat 2 tablespoons of the vegetable oil in wok or large skillet over medium-high heat. Add ½ of eggplant and cook, stirring often, until soft and moist, about 5 minutes. Remove to a colander to drain. Repeat, using 2 more tablespoons vegetable oil and the remaining eggplant.

4. Heat remaining 1 tablespoon vegetable oil in wok over medium-high heat. Add onion-garlic mixture and stir-fry 30 seconds, Return eggplant to wok. Add chicken broth mixture. Bring to a boil and cook, stirring occasionally, until liquid is almost evaporated.

5. Blend water and cornstarch in small cup; add to wok. Cook and stir until sauce boils and thickens slightly. Stir in sesame oil. Garnish with reserved onion slices.

Makes 4 to 5 servings

1

2

3

Shrimp-Stuffed Bean Curd

SHRIMP STUFFING

- 4 ounces shrimp, shelled, deveined and finely chopped
- 2 tablespoons minced water chestnuts
- 2 teaspoons minced green onions
- 1 teaspoon dry sherry
- 1 teaspoon cornstarch
- ½ teaspoon sesame oil
- ¼ teaspoon salt

BEAN CURD

- 1 package (about 1 pound) bean curd
- 3 tablespoons vegetable oil, divided
- 1 cup chicken broth
- 1 tablespoon soy sauce
- ½ teaspoon sugar
- ½ teaspoon fresh ginger
- ½ small head napa cabbage, cut into 2-inch squares
- ½ cup straw mushrooms
- ¼ cup thawed frozen peas
- 1 tablespoon cornstarch
- 1 tablespoon water

1. Combine all shrimp stuffing ingredients in medium bowl; mix well.

2. Drain bean curd. Cut bean curd crosswise through the middle to make 8 triangles. Place between paper towels and gently press out excess water.

3. Cut a pocket in longest side of each triangle. Scoop out ½-inch hole with spoon or knife. Fill hole with 1 tablespoon shrimp filling. Smooth top.

4. Heat 2 tablespoons of the oil in wok or large nonstick skillet over medium heat. Add stuffed bean curd triangles, flat-side down. Cook until golden brown, about 3 minutes on each side. Stand triangles in wok and cook filled-side down 30 seconds. Remove and set aside. Discard drippings; wipe wok clean with paper towels.

5. Combine chicken broth, soy sauce and sugar in small bowl. Heat remaining 1 tablespoon oil in wok over medium-high heat. Add ginger and stir-fry 10 seconds. Add cabbage; stir-fry until cabbage begins to wilt, about 2 minutes. Arrange bean curd triangles on top of cabbage. Sprinkle with straw mushrooms and peas.

6. Pour chicken broth mixture over bean curd. Cover and bring just to a boil; reduce heat and simmer 10 minutes. Blend cornstarch and water in small cup. Gently push bean curd to one side of wok; stir cornstarch mixture into liquid. Cook, stirring carefully, until sauce boils and thickens. *Makes 4 servings*

Ma-Po Bean Curd

1 tablespoon Szechuan
   peppercorns, optional
¾ cup chicken broth
1 tablespoon soy sauce
1 tablespoon dry sherry
2 tablespoons vegetable oil
4 ounces ground pork
2 teaspoons minced fresh
   ginger
2 cloves garlic, minced
1 tablespoon hot bean sauce
12 to 14 ounces bean curd,
   drained and cut into
   ½-inch cubes
2 green onions, thinly sliced
3 tablespoons water
1½ tablespoons cornstarch
1 teaspoon sesame oil

1. Place peppercorns in small dry skillet; shake over medium-low heat, until fragrant, about 2 minutes. Let cool. Crush peppercorns with mortar and pestle or place between paper towels and crush with hammer.*

2. Combine chicken broth, soy sauce and sherry in small bowl.

3. Heat vegetable oil in wok or large skillet over high heat. Add pork and stir-fry until pork is no longer pink, about 2 minutes. Add ginger, garlic and hot bean sauce. Stir-fry until meat absorbs color from bean sauce, about 1 minute.

4. Add chicken broth mixture and bean curd to wok. Simmer, uncovered, 5 minutes. Stir in onions. Blend water and cornstarch in small cup. Add to wok; cook and stir until sauce boils and thickens slightly. Stir in sesame oil. Pass ground peppercorns separately to sprinkle over each serving, if desired.

Makes 3 to 4 servings

*Note: Szechuan peppercorns are deceptively potent. Wear rubber or plastic gloves when crushing them and do not touch eyes or lips when handling.

Bean Curd with Oyster Sauce

2 tablespoons vegetable oil,
   divided
8 ounces bean curd, cut into
   ½-inch cubes
½ cup water
2 tablespoons oyster sauce
1 tablespoon cornstarch
4 teaspoons dry sherry
4 teaspoons soy sauce
4 ounces fresh mushrooms,
   sliced
6 green onions, cut into 1-inch
   pieces
3 stalks celery, diagonally cut
   into ½-inch pieces
1 red or green bell pepper, cut
   into ½-inch chunks

1. Heat 1 tablespoon of the oil in wok or large skillet over high heat. Add bean curd and stir-fry until light brown, about 3 minutes. Remove and set aside. Combine water, oyster sauce, cornstarch, sherry and soy sauce in small bowl.

2. Heat remaining 1 tablespoon oil in wok over high heat. Add all vegetables; stir-fry 1 minute.

3. Return bean curd to wok; toss lightly to combine. Add cornstarch-soy mixture to wok. Cook and stir until liquid boils; cook 1 minute more.   *Makes 4 servings*

Chinese Mixed Pickled Vegetables

PICKLING LIQUID
- 3 cups sugar
- 3 cups distilled white vinegar
- 1½ cups water
- 1½ teaspoons salt

VEGETABLES
- 3 large carrots, cut into 2-inch long thin strips
- 1 large Chinese white radish (about 1 pound), cut into 2-inch long thin strips
- 1 large cucumber, seeded and cut into 2-inch long thin strips
- 4 stalks celery, diagonally cut into ½-inch pieces
- 8 green onions, diagonally cut into ¼-inch pieces
- 4 ounces fresh ginger, pared and thinly sliced
- 1 large red bell pepper, cut into ½-inch cubes
- 1 large green bell pepper, cut into ½-inch cubes

1. Combine all pickling liquid ingredients in 3-quart saucepan. Bring to a boil, stirring, over medium heat. Cool.

2. For vegetables, fill 5-quart stockpot or Dutch oven ½ full of water. Bring to a boil and add all vegetables. Remove from heat and let stand 2 minutes.

3. Drain vegetables in large colander. Spread vegetables out on clean towels; allow to dry 2 to 3 hours.

4. Pack vegetables firmly into clean jars with tight-fitting lids. Pour Pickling Liquid into jars to cover vegetables. Seal jars tightly. Store in refrigerator at least 1 week before using.
Makes 1½ to 2 quarts

Rice & Noodles

Fried Rice

3 cups water
1½ teaspoons salt
1½ cups long-grain rice
4 slices bacon, chopped
3 eggs
⅛ teaspoon pepper
3 tablespoons vegetable oil, divided
2 teaspoons minced fresh ginger
8 ounces Barbecued Pork (page 11), cut into thin strips
8 ounces cooked shrimp, shelled, deveined and coarsely chopped
8 green onions, finely chopped
1 to 2 tablespoons soy sauce

1. Combine water and salt in 3-quart saucepan. Cover and bring to a boil. Stir in rice; reduce heat, cover and simmer until rice is tender, 15 to 20 minutes; drain.

2. Cook bacon in wok over medium heat, stirring often, until crisp; drain. Remove all but 1 tablespoon bacon drippings from wok.

3. Beat eggs and pepper with fork in small bowl. Pour ⅓ of egg mixture into wok. Tilt wok slightly so egg covers bottom. Cook over medium heat until eggs are set, 1 to 2 minutes. Remove from wok. Roll up omelet and cut into thin strips. Pour ½ tablespoon of the oil into wok. Add ½ of remaining egg mixture; tilt wok and cook until eggs are set. Remove, roll up and cut into thin strips. Repeat with another ½ tablespoon oil and remaining eggs.

4. Heat remaining 2 tablespoons oil in wok over medium-high heat. Add ginger and stir-fry 1 minute. Add rice; cook and stir 5 minutes. Stir in eggs, bacon, pork, shrimp, onions and soy sauce. Cook and stir until heated through.

Makes 6 to 8 servings

Steamed Rice

1 cup long-grain rice
2 cups water
1 teaspoon salt
1 tablespoon vegetable oil

1. Place rice in strainer and rinse under cold running water to remove excess starch. Combine rice, water, salt and oil in 3-quart saucepan.

2. Cook over medium-high heat until water boils. Reduce heat to low, cover and simmer until rice is tender, 15 to 20 minutes.

3. Remove from heat; let stand 5 minutes. Uncover and fluff rice lightly with fork. *Makes 3 cups*

1

2

Vegetarian Fried Rice

4 dried mushrooms
4 cups cooked long-grain rice
3 eggs
¾ teaspoon salt, divided
2½ tablespoons vegetable oil, divided
1 teaspoon minced fresh ginger
1 clove garlic, minced
3 green onions, thinly sliced
4 ounces bean curd, deep fried and cut into ¼-inch cubes
1 tablespoon soy sauce
¼ teaspoon sugar
1 cup bean sprouts, coarsely chopped
½ cup thawed frozen peas

1. Place mushrooms in small bowl and cover with hot water. Let stand 30 minutes. Drain, reserving liquid. Squeeze out excess water. Cut off and discard stems; dice caps.

2. Rub rice with wet hands so all the grains are separated.

3. Beat eggs with ¼ teaspoon of the salt in medium bowl. Heat ½ tablespoon oil in wok or large skillet over medium heat. Add eggs; cook and stir until soft curds form. Remove from heat and cut eggs into small pieces using a spoon. Remove and set aside.

4. Heat remaining 2 tablespoons oil in wok over high heat. Add ginger, garlic and onions; stir-fry 10 seconds. Add mushrooms, ¼ cup of the reserved mushroom soaking liquid, the bean curd, soy sauce and sugar. Cook until most of the liquid evaporates, about 4 minutes. Add bean sprouts and peas; cook 30 seconds.

5. Add rice and remaining ½ teaspoon salt. Stir and toss until heated through. Add a few drops mushroom soaking liquid if rice appears dry. Fold in eggs before serving.

Makes 4 servings

Noodles with Simmered Chicken ᴤᴤᴤᴤᴤᴤᴤᴤᴤᴤᴤᴤᴤ

4 dried mushrooms
2 teaspoons dry sherry
1 boneless, skinless chicken
    breast half, thinly sliced
1 small bunch watercress or
    ½ bunch fresh spinach
    leaves
8 ounces Chinese-style thin egg
    noodles
2 cups chicken broth
1 tablespoon soy sauce
¼ cup sliced bamboo shoots
1 teaspoon sesame oil
    Dash ground white pepper
2 green onions, thinly sliced

1. Place mushrooms in bowl and cover with hot water. Let stand 30 minutes. Drain and squeeze out ex-cess water. Cut off and discard stems; cut caps into thin slices.

2. Sprinkle sherry over chicken slices in medium bowl; let stand 15 minutes.

3. Wash watercress and discard thick stems. If using spinach, wash and remove stems; cut into 2-inch wide strips.

4. Cook noodles according to package directions until tender but still firm, 2 to 3 minutes. Drain, rinse under cold running water and drain again.

5. Bring chicken broth and soy sauce to a boil in 3-quart saucepan. Add mushrooms, chicken and bamboo shoots. Reduce heat and simmer, uncovered, about 4 minutes. Add watercress, sesame oil and pepper; simmer 1 minute. Add noodles and cook until heated through.

6. Divide noodles, chicken and vegetables between 2 serving bowls. Ladle broth over noodles. Sprinkle each serving with onions.

Makes 2 servings

Note: To store leftover bamboo shoots, place shoots in jar with tight-fitting lid. Add water to cover and seal jar tightly. Bamboo shoots will keep, refrigerated, for up to 10 days, changing water daily.

Lo Mein Noodles with Shrimp

12 ounces Chinese-style thin egg
  noodles
2 teaspoons sesame oil
1½ tablespoons oyster sauce
1½ tablespoons soy sauce
½ teaspoon sugar
¼ teaspoon salt
¼ teaspoon ground white
  pepper
2 tablespoons vegetable oil
1 teaspoon minced fresh ginger
1 clove garlic, minced
8 ounces medium shrimp,
  shelled and deveined
1 tablespoon dry sherry
½ cup Chinese chives, cut into
  1-inch pieces or ¼ cup
  domestic chives, cut into
  1-inch pieces and 2 green
  onions, cut into 1-inch
  pieces
8 ounces bean sprouts

1. Cook noodles according to package directions until tender but still firm, 2 to 3 minutes. Drain, rinse under cold running water and drain again. Toss noodles with sesame oil until well coated.

2. Combine oyster sauce, soy sauce, sugar, salt and pepper in small bowl.

3. Heat vegetable oil in wok or large skillet over high heat. Add ginger and garlic and stir-fry 10 seconds. Add shrimp; stir-fry until shrimp begin to turn pink, about 1 minute. Add sherry and chives; stir-fry until chives begin to wilt, about 15 seconds. Add ½ of bean sprouts; stir-fry 15 seconds. Add remaining bean sprouts; stir-fry 15 seconds more.

4. Add oyster sauce mixture and noodles. Cook and stir until heated through, about 2 minutes.

Makes 4 servings

1

4

Cold Stirred Noodles

DRESSING
6 tablespoons soy sauce
2 tablespoons sesame oil
¼ cup red wine vinegar
2½ tablespoons sugar
¼ to ½ teaspoon chili oil
    (or to taste)

NOODLES
1 pound Chinese-style thin egg
    noodles
1 tablespoon sesame oil
2 small carrots, cut into 3-inch
    pieces and shredded
3 cups bean sprouts
½ large thin-skinned cucumber,
    cut into 3-inch pieces and
    shredded
1 bunch radishes, shredded
4 green onions, cut into 2-inch
    slivers
1 cup matchstick strips
    Barbecued Pork (page 11),
    optional

1. Combine all dressing ingredients in small bowl; mix well.

2. Cut noodles into 6-inch pieces. Cook noodles according to package directions until tender but still firm, 2 to 3 minutes. Drain, rinse under cold running water and drain again. Toss noodles with sesame oil until well coated. Refrigerate until ready to serve.

3. Cook carrots in pot of boiling water 30 seconds; drain and rinse under cold running water. Cook bean sprouts in boiling water 30 seconds; drain and rinse under cold running water.

4. To serve, arrange noodles on large platter. Arrange all remaining vegetables and pork on top; sprinkle with onions. Pass dressing separately.

Makes 6 to 8 servings

1

2

Vermicelli

**8 ounces Chinese rice vermicelli
or bean threads
Vegetable oil for frying**

1. Cut bundle of vermicelli in half. Gently pull each half apart into small bunches.

2. Heat oil in wok or large skillet over medium-high heat to 375°F. Using tongs or slotted spoon, lower a small bunch of vermicelli into hot oil. Cook until vermicelli rises to top, 3 to 5 seconds. Immediately remove and drain on paper towels. Repeat with remaining bunches.

Makes about 4 servings

1

2

2

Bean Threads with Minced Pork ～～～～～～～～

4 ounces bean threads or
   Chinese rice vermicelli
3 dried mushrooms
1 small red or green hot chili
   pepper
3 green onions
2 tablespoons minced fresh
   ginger
2 tablespoons hot bean sauce
1½ cups chicken broth
1 tablespoon soy sauce
1 tablespoon dry sherry
2 tablespoons vegetable oil
6 ounces lean ground pork
2 cilantro sprigs (Chinese
   parsley), for garnish

1. Place bean threads and dried mushrooms in separate bowls. Cover each with hot water. Let stand 30 minutes; drain. Cut bean threads into 4-inch pieces. Squeeze out excess water from mushrooms. Cut off and discard stems; cut caps into thin slices.

2. Cut chili pepper in half and scrape out seeds.* Finely mince chili pepper. Thinly slice 2 of the green onions. Cut remaining onion into 1½-inch slivers and reserve for garnish. Combine ginger and hot bean sauce in small bowl. Combine chicken broth, soy sauce and sherry in medium bowl.

3. Heat oil in wok or large skillet over high heat. Add pork and stir-fry until meat is no longer pink, about 2 minutes. Add chili pepper, sliced onions and ginger-bean sauce mixture. Stir-fry until meat absorbs color from bean sauce, about 1 minute.

4. Add chicken broth mixture, bean threads and mushrooms. Simmer, uncovered, until most of the liquid is absorbed, about 5 minutes. Garnish with onion slivers and cilantro sprigs.   *Makes 4 servings*

*Note: Wear rubber or plastic gloves when cutting chili peppers. Do not touch eyes or lips when handling.

Fried Noodles

8 ounces Chinese-style thin egg
　noodles
Salt
Vegetable oil for frying

1. Cook noodles according to package directions until tender but still firm, 2 to 3 minutes. Drain, rinse under cold running water and drain again.

2. Place several layers of paper towels over cookie sheets or jelly-roll pans. Spread noodles over paper towels and let dry 2 to 3 hours.

3. Heat oil in wok or large skillet over medium-high heat to 375°F. Using tongs or slotted spoon, lower a small portion of noodles into hot oil. Cook until golden, about 30 seconds. Drain on paper towels. Repeat with remaining noodles.

Makes 4 servings

Beef Chow Mein

1½ pounds beef rump steak
3½ tablespoons soy sauce, divided
3½ tablespoons dry sherry, divided
1 tablespoon satay sauce
12 ounces Chinese-style thin egg noodles
4 tablespoons vegetable oil, divided
¾ cup water
1 tablespoon cornstarch
2½ tablespoons oyster sauce
2 teaspoons instant chicken bouillon granules
2 yellow onions, cut into wedges and separated
3 stalks celery, diagonally cut into ½-inch pieces
4 ounces fresh mushrooms, sliced
1 red or green bell pepper, cut into thin strips
4 ounces bean sprouts

1. Cut meat across the grain into thin slices. Combine 1½ tablespoons of the soy sauce, 1 tablespoon of the sherry and the satay sauce in medium bowl. Add meat and stir to coat well. Cover and refrigerate 1 hour.

2. Cook noodles according to package directions until tender but still firm, 2 to 3 minutes. Drain, rinse under cold running water and drain again. Heat 1 tablespoon of the oil in wok or large skillet over high heat. Add noodles and 1 tablespoon of the soy sauce; stir-fry until lightly browned, about 2 minutes. Transfer to serving plate; keep warm.

3. Blend water, cornstarch, oyster sauce, bouillon, remaining 2½ tablespoons sherry and 1 tablespoon soy sauce in small bowl.

4. Heat 1 tablespoon of the oil in wok over high heat. Add onions and stir-fry 1 minute. Add celery, mushrooms, red pepper and sprouts; stir-fry 2 minutes. Remove and set aside.

5. Heat remaining 2 tablespoons oil in wok over high heat. Add beef and stir-fry until browned, about 5 minutes. Stir in water mixture; cover and cook 3 minutes. Return vegetables to wok. Cook and stir until heated through, 1 to 2 minutes more. Spoon mixture over noodles.

Makes 4 to 6 servings

1

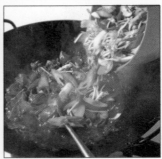

4

Chicken Chow Mein

Fried Noodles (page 111)
2½ tablespoons dry sherry, divided
2 tablespoons soy sauce, divided
3 teaspoons cornstarch, divided
2 whole boneless, skinless chicken breasts, cut into 1-inch pieces
8 ounces boneless lean pork, cut into 1-inch pieces
½ cup water
2 teaspoons instant chicken bouillon granules
2 tablespoons vegetable oil
1 piece fresh ginger (1 inch square), pared and finely chopped
1 clove garlic, crushed
8 ounces shelled, deveined shrimp
2 medium yellow onions, chopped
1 red or green bell pepper, thinly sliced
2 stalks celery, diagonally cut into 1-inch slices
8 green onions, chopped
4 ounces cabbage (¼ of small head), shredded

1. Prepare Fried Noodles; set aside.

2. Blend ½ tablespoon of the sherry, ½ tablespoon of the soy sauce and 1 teaspoon of the cornstarch in large bowl. Add chicken and pork; toss to coat well. Cover and refrigerate 1 hour.

3. Combine water, bouillon granules, remaining 2 teaspoons cornstarch, 2 tablespoons sherry and 1½ tablespoons soy sauce in small bowl; set aside. Heat oil in wok or large skillet over high heat. Add ginger and garlic and stir-fry 1 minute. Add chicken and pork; stir-fry until pork is no longer pink, about 5 minutes. Add shrimp; stir-fry until shrimp turn pink, about 3 minutes.

4. Add all vegetables to wok. Stir-fry until vegetables are crisp-tender, 3 to 5 minutes. Add bouillon-soy sauce mixture to wok. Cook and stir until sauce boils and thickens, then cook and stir 1 minute more.

5. Arrange Fried Noodles on serving plate; spoon chow mein over noodles.   *Makes 6 servings*

4

Desserts

Chinese cuisine does not offer a wide range of desserts. We have included a few traditional recipes in this section, and have added some light and lovely desserts which would make a superb ending to a Chinese meal.

Watermelon in Ginger Wine

½ watermelon
1 cup water
½ cup ginger wine
2 tablespoons sugar
1 ounce preserved candied
   ginger

1. Using a rounded melon baller, cut melon balls from top surface of watermelon, removing seeds as necessary. When all of the top has been used, cut off rind using long sharp knife. Scoop out remaining watermelon.

2. Place melon balls in large bowl. Combine water, wine and sugar in small saucepan. Cook over medium heat, stirring until sugar dissolves and mixture is hot. Remove from heat.

3. Cut ginger into thin slivers. Stir into ginger wine mixture. Pour over melon balls. Refrigerate several hours or overnight, stirring occasionally.

4. Spoon melon balls and wine mixture into serving bowls.

Makes 4 to 6 servings

Almond Creme

1 envelope unflavored gelatin
¾ cup cold water
½ cup sugar
¾ cup boiling water
1¼ cups evaporated milk
½ teaspoon vanilla extract
½ teaspoon almond extract
2 kiwi fruits, optional
4 fresh ripe strawberries,
    optional

1. Sprinkle gelatin over cold water in small bowl; let stand 1 minute to soften.

2. Add sugar to gelatin mixture; stir until gelatin dissolves. Pour boiling water into medium bowl; stir in gelatin mixture.

3. Stir milk, vanilla and almond extracts into gelatin mixture. Divide mixture between 4 serving dishes. Refrigerate until set, about 3 hours.

4. Peel and slice kiwi fruit. Arrange kiwi and strawberries over each serving, if desired.   *Makes 4 servings*

Banana Fritters

1½ cups all-purpose flour, divided
1 teaspoon baking powder
¼ teaspoon baking soda
¼ teaspoon salt
¾ cup water
4 firm bananas
Vegetable oil for frying
Vanilla ice cream, optional

1. Combine 1 cup of the flour, the baking powder, soda and salt in large bowl.

2. Gradually blend in water, beating with whisk until smooth.

3. Cut each banana crosswise into 3 pieces, yielding 12 pieces total. Coat bananas lightly with remaining ½ cup flour.

4. Heat oil in wok or large skillet over high heat to 375°F. Dip banana pieces in flour-water mixture, coating well. Cook 4 to 6 banana pieces at a time until golden, 3 to 5 minutes. Drain on paper towels. Serve with vanilla ice cream, if desired.

Makes 4 servings

2

3

4

Lychees and Mandarin Ice

2 cups water
½ cup sugar
2 cans (11 ounces each) mandarin orange segments
¼ cup lemon juice
2 tablespoons orange-flavored liqueur
1 can (20 ounces) peeled whole lychees

1. Combine water and sugar in medium saucepan. Bring to a boil over low heat, stirring constantly. Boil and stir 3 minutes. Remove from heat; cool.

2. Place one can of mandarin oranges with syrup in blender or food processor. Process until smooth, about 1 minute. Strain mixture.

3. Stir blended oranges, lemon juice and liqueur into cooled sugar mixture. Pour into 1½-quart rectangular pan or dish. Freeze until firm, at least 3 hours.

4. Refrigerate lychees and remaining mandarin oranges until well chilled.

5. To serve, drain lychees, reserving syrup; drain oranges. Spoon fruit and lychee syrup into serving dishes.

6. Flake frozen fruit mixture with fork or spoon over fruit in each dish.   *Makes 4 servings*

1

2

3

1   3 \   5

Melon with Champagne ⌇⌇⌇⌇⌇⌇⌇⌇⌇⌇⌇⌇⌇⌇⌇⌇⌇⌇⌇

1 small honeydew melon
½ cup water
½ cup sugar
¼ cup ginger wine
1 bottle (750ml) champagne
1 pound seedless green grapes
1 egg white
1 cup super-fine granulated
    sugar

1. Cut melon in half and remove seeds. Using a rounded melon baller, cut melon balls from honeydew. Place melon balls in large bowl, cover with plastic wrap and refrigerate until well chilled.

2. Combine water, sugar and wine in small saucepan. Bring to a boil over medium heat, stirring until sugar dissolves; boil 3 minutes. Remove from heat and refrigerate until cold. Refrigerate champagne until cold.

3. Cut grapes into 6 small bunches, leaving a large enough stem section on each to hook over rim of a glass.

4. Beat egg white in small bowl with fork until frothy. Brush grapes with egg white.

5. Immediately place grapes in sugar, turning to coat completely. Place grapes on large plate and let stand 2 hours.

6. Divide melon balls between 6 large wine glasses. Spoon about 2 tablespoons ginger-syrup mixture over melon in each glass. Fill glasses with champagne. Hang a bunch of frosted grapes over outside edge of each glass.   *Makes 6 servings*

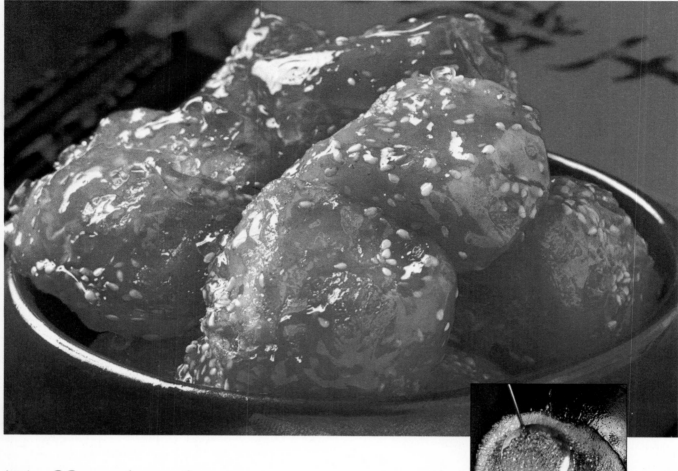

Toffee Apples ~~~~~~~~~~~~~~~~~~~~~~

2 medium green cooking apples, such as Granny Smith, peeled and cut into quarters
1 cup all-purpose flour
2 cups water, divided
3 teaspoons sesame oil, divided
Vegetable oil for frying
2 cups sugar
2 tablespoons sesame seeds
Cold water
Ice cubes

1. Cut each apple quarter in half crosswise to yield 16 pieces total.

2. Place flour in large bowl. Blend in 1 cup of the water using a whisk. Add 2 teaspoons of the sesame oil; beat until smooth.

3. Brush a serving plate with remaining 1 teaspoon sesame oil. Set aside.

4. Add apple pieces to batter; stir to coat well.

5. Heat vegetable oil in wok or large skillet over medium-high heat to 375°F. Using a slotted spoon, lift about ½ the apple pieces at a time from batter and add to wok. Cook until light brown, about 2 minutes. Drain on paper towels.

6. Remove oil from wok; do not clean out wok. Pour remaining 1 cup water and sugar into wok. Cook, stirring constantly, until mixture reaches about 235°F on a candy thermometer (soft ball stage), 10 to 13 minutes.

7. Remove from heat immediately. Stir in apples and sesame seeds. Transfer to oiled serving plate. Place cold water and ice cubes in medium bowl. Dunk apples in ice water before eating.   *Makes 4 servings*

5

7

7

Strawberry Sorbet

1 pint fresh strawberries,
  washed and hulled
1 cup water
¾ cup super-fine granulated
  sugar, divided
2½ tablespoons lemon juice
2½ tablespoons orange-flavored
  liqueur
2 egg whites
¼ teaspoon cream of tartar
  Watermelon, cut into 1-inch
  pieces, optional

1. Place strawberries, water, ½ cup of the sugar, the lemon juice and liqueur in 5-cup blender container. Blend until smooth, about 2 minutes.

2. Pour strawberry mixture through strainer into an 11×7-inch baking pan. Freeze until firm, 3 to 4 hours.

3. Beat egg whites and cream of tartar in large bowl until frothy. Add remaining ¼ cup sugar, 1 tablespoon at a time, beating constantly until sugar is dissolved and stiff peaks form.

4. Remove strawberry mixture from freezer. Flake with a fork. Spoon beaten egg whites over strawberry mixture. Gently but thoroughly fold whites into strawberry mixture. Freeze until firm, about 2 hours.

5. Spoon into serving dishes over watermelon.   *Makes 6 servings*

1   2   3   4

Custard Tarts

3 cups all-purpose flour
1 teaspoon salt, divided
1 cup vegetable shortening or lard
4 to 6 tablespoons hot water
3 eggs
⅓ cup sugar
1½ cups milk

1. Combine flour and ½ teaspoon of the salt in large bowl. Cut in shortening until mixture resembles bread crumbs. Mix in enough water to form a dough that sticks together. Shape dough into a ball; cut ball in half.

2. Roll out each half on lightly floured work surface to ⅛-inch thickness. Cut 12 circles from each half using a 3-inch diameter fluted cookie cutter.

3. Fit pastry circles into greased muffin cups, pressing sides so they reach rims.

4. Beat eggs with whisk. Stir in sugar and remaining ½ teaspoon salt. Gradually blend in milk. Spoon about 2 tablespoons egg mixture into each pastry cup.

5. Bake in preheated 350°F oven until knife inserted in center of custards comes out clean, 25 to 30 minutes. Remove tarts from pans. Cool on wire racks. *Makes 2 dozen*

1   1   3   4

Chocolate Ginger Lychees

1 can (20 ounces) whole peeled lychees
2 ounces preserved candied ginger
6 ounces semi-sweet baking chocolate (6 squares)
1 tablespoon vegetable shortening

1. Drain lychees. Spread lychees round-side up between several layers of paper towels. Let stand until dry, about 1 hour.

2. Cut ginger into slivers or tiny pieces. Carefully stuff ginger inside cavities of lychees.

3. Combine chocolate and shortening in small saucepan in top of double boiler over boiling water. Cook over low heat, stirring constantly, just until chocolate melts. Remove from heat; cool slightly.

4. Dip each lychee into chocolate mixture to coat completely. Carefully lift lychee out of chocolate and place round-side up on waxed paper. Drizzle remaining chocolate over lychees. Refrigerate until cold.

Makes about 2 dozen

1

1

3

3

Sesame Peanut Candy ᠌᠌᠌᠌᠌᠌᠌᠌᠌᠌᠌᠌᠌᠌᠌᠌᠌᠌᠌᠌᠌᠌᠌᠌᠌᠌᠌᠌᠌᠌᠌᠌᠌᠌

2 cups sugar
⅓ cup distilled white vinegar
4 teaspoons water
½ cup sesame seeds, toasted*
1½ cups roasted unsalted, skinless peanuts (about 8 ounces)

1. Combine sugar, vinegar and water in medium saucepan. Cook over low heat, stirring just until sugar dissolves. Cook without stirring until mixture boils. Boil mixture without stirring until golden and reaches 295°F to 300°F, or hard-crack stage, on a candy thermometer, about 10 minutes.

2. While sugar mixture is boiling, grease 11×7×1½-inch baking pan. Sprinkle half of the sesame seeds and all of the peanuts into pan.

3. Pour sugar mixture over nuts in pan. Smooth surface with back of a wooden spoon. Sprinkle with remaining sesame seeds. Cool slightly. While candy is still warm, cut into 2×1-inch pieces. Cool completely. Remove from pan.

Makes 2½ to 3 dozen pieces

*Note: To toast sesame seeds, sprinkle seeds into 11×7×1½-inch baking pan. Bake in preheated 350°F oven until golden, about 5 minutes. Cool.

China Tea

For over a thousand years tea has been the drink of China. The Chinese drink it morning, noon and night; before, during and after meals. They never interfere with tea's natural flavor by adding sugar, lemon, cream or milk.

VARIETIES OF CHINESE TEA

There are many varieties of Chinese tea that differ greatly in character, flavor and aroma. Because the leaves for all Chinese teas come from the same plant (a member of the camellia family), the differences are a result of processing techniques.

Green Tea: an unfermented tea that produces a light golden brew. Its leaves retain their natural green color and its flavor is delicate. It's is suitable for drinking day and night with most foods.

Black Tea: a fermented tea that produces a full bodied brew. Its leaves change color during fermentation from green to red to black. It's a good choice for accompanying full-flavored, spicy dishes and deep fried foods. Among black teas, the most popular include Keemun and Lapsang Souchong.

Oolong Tea: a semi-fermented tea that yields an amber brew. It combines the more pungent aroma of the black teas and the delicate fragrance of the green teas. The fermentation process is stopped midway, producing leaves that are brownish-green. Oolong tea is a good choice with distinctively flavored foods such as shrimp, fish, broccoli and cauliflower.

Scented Tea: a blend of tea leaves and fresh or dried flowers. Scented teas can be made from green, black or oolong varieties. They are good with many stir-fried dishes and are especially nice between meals. The most popular scented teas are jasmine, lychee and chrysanthemum.

BREWING CHINA TEA

There is no exact recipe for making Chinese teas. The amount required to brew a cup varies with the variety and nature of each tea. Unlike many other teas, the color of Chinese tea is not a good indicator of its strength of flavor. (It is usually stronger than its color suggests.) A general guideline is to use ½ to 1 teaspoon tea for each 1 cup of water. Green teas are more potent than other varieties and should be used in smaller amounts.

Tea is generally made in a teapot — a china one, as opposed to metal — that must be clean. To brew the tea, scald the inside of the pot with boiling water (only freshly drawn water should be used), then discard the water. Add tea leaves to the pot. Pour in more boiling water. Cover the pot. Let it steep 3 to 5 minutes (time the brewing). Do not attempt to judge doneness by its color. If brewing tea in a cup, follow the same procedure, placing the leaves in the bottom of a cup.

Most Chinese teas can be brewed (infused) more than once. In fact, many believe that the flavor of the second infusion is superior to the first. The second brewing is done exactly like the first, without adding more tea leaves.

Index